Thinking Like an Engineer

THINKING LIKE AN ENGINEER

GRADE 4

Lessons That Develop Habits of Mind and Thinking Skills for Young Engineers

DEBBIE DAILEY, ED.D.

Routledge
Taylor & Francis Group
NEW YORK AND LONDON

First published in 2019 by Prufrock.Press Inc.

Published in 2021 by Routledge
605 Third Avenue, New York, NY 10017
2 Park Square, Milton Park, Abingdon, Oxon OX14 4RN

Routledge is an imprint of the Taylor & Francis Group, an informa business.

© 2019 by Taylor & Francis Group

Cover design and layout design by Micah Benson

Notice:
Product or corporate names may be trademarks or registered trademarks, and are used only for identification and explanation without intent to infringe.

ISBN: 9781032141800 (hbk)
ISBN: 9781618218285 (pbk)

DOI: 10.4324/9781003239093

TABLE OF CONTENTS

INTRODUCTION

PURPOSE

Thinking Like an Engineer is a curriculum unit designed to engage students in design thinking while teaching them about multiple engineering career options. The Next Generation Science Standards (NGSS Lead States, 2013) encourage teachers to use the engineering design process (Engineering is Elementary, 2018a) as an instructional approach to teaching science. In *A Framework for K–12 Science Education*, the precursor to the NGSS, the National Research Council (NRC, 2012) stressed that the increased emphasis on engineering was not intended to develop more engineers. However, the NRC maintained that

> students should have gained sufficient knowledge of the practices, crosscutting concepts, and core ideas of science and engineering to engage in public discussions on science-related issues, to be critical consumers of scientific information related to their everyday lives, and to continue to learn about science throughout their lives. (p. 12)

Using the five-step engineering design process (i.e., Ask, Imagine, Plan, Create, Improve; see Figure 1) as an instructional strategy puts a focus on real-world problem solving while students actively engage in learning content across multiple disciplines (Dailey, 2017; Engineering is Elementary, 2018a). Teachers often assume that engineering is most appropriate when integrated with mathematics or science; however, the engineering design process can be used with any content area or domain to engage students in critical and creative problem solving. For example, students can use the engineering design process to solve problems found in fiction or nonfiction stories in an ELA lesson or unit. In a social studies lesson, students might use the steps to design a plan to improve living conditions in an impoverished area. Furthermore, "knowledge is built as students progress through the

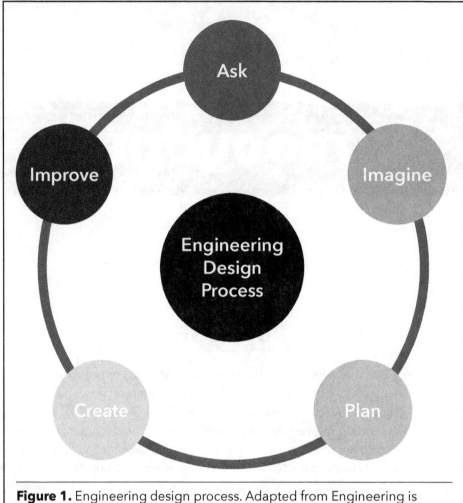

Figure 1. Engineering design process. Adapted from Engineering is Elementary, 2018a.

challenges and content is provided on a *need to know basis*; thereby, differentiating instruction based on learner needs" (Dailey, 2017, p. 138).

Using the engineering design process as an instructional approach or model prepares students for problem solving outside the context of the classroom. With ever-changing technologies, students need to be active and practiced problem solvers and innovative thinkers. Utilizing this approach with real-world problems helps students prepare for advances in the future. In a world where content is at their fingertips, teaching students to critically and creatively solve problems is vital.

ORGANIZATION OF THE BOOK

Unit 1 introduces students to engineers and their characteristics, job roles, and careers. The unit concludes with a challenge to engage students in design thinking using the engineering design process.

Unit 2 provides students opportunities to learn about the branches of engineering and how to become an engineer. A focus in this unit is granting students opportunities to interact with practicing engineers through virtual or face-to-face field trips, guest speakers, or video (e.g., Skype) sessions.

Units 3–5 immerse students in the practices of engineers. Each unit is based on a theme: Design Cities Like an Engineer, Care for Your World Like an Engineer, and Explore Beyond Your World Like an Engineer. In each unit, students will solve real-world problems using the engineering design process: Ask, Imagine, Plan, Create, and Improve. There are eight challenges included in these units. You may elect to complete each challenge (or unit), select particular challenges for the class to complete, or allow groups of students to choose which challenges they would like to do.

Unit 6 gives students the opportunity to demonstrate their learning. Students are encouraged to share and communicate their engineering solutions to a formal audience in the format of their choice. Students will then complete and present activities chosen from a tic-tac-toe board to represent their learning progress. Unit 6 concludes with students organizing and presenting a living museum. Each student will embody an engineer from one of the branches of engineering.

ASSESSMENTS

I encourage the use of pre- and postassessments to guide instructional paths for students and measure student progress. Engineering is Elementary (2018b) has developed instruments to measure students' interest and attitudes about engineering as well as their knowledge of engineering (see https://www.eie.org/engineering-elementary/research/research-instruments). I recommend that teachers review these instruments.

Figure 2 is a sample checklist that can be used by teachers during the design challenges. This checklist could easily be converted to a rubric to assess different levels of proficiency. Additionally, each lesson in each unit has a set of Assessment Observations to guide formative assessment strategies.

	Requirements	Yes/No
Ask	Students asked questions to determine the constraints and criteria of the challenge.	
Imagine	Students brainstormed in their groups to discuss possible solutions to their problem. Students listened to other group members' ideas and did not dominate the conversation.	
Plan	Students produced a detailed plan of their proposed design, utilizing ideas from all group members.	
Create	Students utilized available resources to construct a prototype or model for their design. Students conducted controlled experiments when appropriate to determine the effectiveness of their design.	
Improve	Students improved their design using data from fair tests and recommendations from others. Students presented their completed designs to formal audiences.	

Figure 2. Engineering design process checklist.

When possible, students should conduct controlled experiments when testing their products. Controlled experiments involve the experimenter controlling for other factors that may impact the results. Everything is treated exactly the same except for the substance being tested. The following definitions should be used.

- **Independent Variable:** The variable that is changed by the experimenter.
- **Dependent Variable:** The variable that is changed as a result of the independent variable.
- **Control:** When the independent variable is not changed; the experimenter compares what happens in the control with what happens in the experiment.
- **Constant:** What is kept the same in the experiment.

STANDARDS

The national standards used in each unit can be found in the standards alignment sections of the book. This book uses the Common Core State Standards (Mathematics and English Language Arts) and the Next Generation Science Standards (NGSS). Depending on teacher direction and student needs, additional standards could be addressed. For example, when constructing the tower in Lesson 1.3, you could integrate appropriate science and mathematics content dealing with forces and motion, balance, geometry, measurement and estimation, problem solving, etc.

THINKING LIKE SERIES

This book is one in a series, developed in conjunction with the Center for Gifted Education at William & Mary, intended to develop process skills in various content areas and enhance discipline-specific thinking and habits of mind through hands-on activities. Each book in the series focuses on a specific discipline and grade level.

- In *Thinking Like a Geographer*, students in grade 2 develop and practice geography skills, such as reading and creating maps, graphs, and charts; examine primary and secondary sources; and think spatially on a variety of scales.

- In *Thinking Like a Mathematician*, students in grade 3 engage in exploration activities, complete mathematical challenges, and then apply what they have learned by making real-world connections.

- In *Thinking Like an Engineer*, students in grade 4 complete design challenges, visit with an engineer, and investigate real-world problems to plan feasible engineering solutions.

- In *Thinking Like a Scientist*, students in grade 5 use inquiry-based investigations to explore what scientists do, engage in critical thinking, learn about scientific tools and research, and examine careers in scientific fields.

UNIT 1
WHAT IS AN ENGINEER?

RATIONALE

The unit will familiarize students with engineers and their characteristics, job roles, and careers. The unit concludes with an introduction to design thinking using the engineering design process.

PLAN

In Lesson 1.1, students will complete a Draw an Engineer Test. This assessment should be readministered after Unit 6 is completed to examine the progress made by students. After completing the test, students will complete a Frayer model in order to develop a definition of an engineer.

In Lesson 1.2, students will read a biography about an engineer. Throughout the unit, students should remember and compare the characteristics of the real-life engineer to their own characteristics as they solve various problems.

In Lesson 1.3, students will be introduced to the engineering design process on a "need to know" basis. Students will be given a challenge to solve before they are provided information about the engineering design process. After completing the challenge, students will reflect on and discuss how their design/solution could be better and what they need to improve it.

LESSON 1.1

WHAT IS AN ENGINEER?

RESOURCES AND MATERIALS

- Lesson 1.1 Draw an Engineer Test
- Sticky notes
- Chart paper with blank Frayer model
- Video: "Solve Problems: Be an Engineer!" (https://www.youtube.com/watch?v=D9I35Rqo04E)

ESTIMATED TIME

60–75 minutes

OBJECTIVES

In this lesson students will:
- illustrate an engineer,
- compare and contrast various illustrations of engineers,
- evaluate roles and characteristics of engineers, and
- develop a definition of an engineer.

CONTENT

The purpose of the Draw an Engineer Test (Knight & Cunningham, 2004) is to understand and use students' preconceived ideas to help guide instruction. Typically, students will draw engineers as men who fix things.

Working with the Frayer model will allow students to examine the roles and characteristics of engineers through brainstorming, discussion, and structured argument.

PRIOR KNOWLEDGE

Skills: compare and contrast, data collection, presentation tools
Vocabulary: engineer, characteristics, example, nonexample, career

INSTRUCTIONAL SEQUENCE

1. Distribute Lesson 1.1 Draw an Engineer Test to determine students' existing perceptions of engineers. Instruct students to draw an engineer in an engineer's work environment. You may ask: *What does an engineer do? What does an engineer look like?*

2. After students complete the drawing, divide them into groups of 3–4. Instruct students to compare and contrast their drawings with their group members' by completing the graphic organizer included in Lesson 1.1 Draw an Engineer Test.

3. Have students create a list of shared characteristics that they can all agree on. Students should then develop a new drawing based on their group's consensus. These revised drawings could be completed using regular paper or poster-sized paper. Alternately, students could complete this exercise using a computer or tablet drawing application, such as Sketchpad.

4. Display the new drawings, and ask groups to participate in a gallery walk, noting how other groups' drawings are similar and different.

5. As an alternative to creating a new drawing, students could use an app such as HP Reveal to create a video about an engineer. The original drawing would launch the video; during the gallery walk, students could access the video through the app.

6. Once students have completed their gallery walk, present the video "Solve Problems: Be an Engineer."

7. Present a class Frayer model created on chart paper or projected on the board (see Figure 3). In groups of 3–4, students should list roles and tasks of an engineer on sticky notes. Have students add their sticky notes to the class Frayer model.

8. As a class, have students categorize engineering roles and tasks based on identified and agreed-upon criteria. Although students have not yet learned about the engineering design process, look for students to form criteria such as "engineers ask questions," "engineers create and improve," etc.

9. In their groups, have students list examples of engineering titles or jobs (e.g., chemical engineer, electrical engineer, etc.). Have students add their examples to the class Frayer model.

10. Conduct a debate in which students discuss whether or not the examples are correct. For example, students might ask, "Is there an engineer called a virtual reality engineer?" (A virtual reality engineer is a software engineer specializing in virtual reality.)

11. In their groups, instruct students to list nonexamples of engineer jobs, such as accountants, bankers, and actors. Have students add their nonexamples to the class Frayer model poster or drawing.

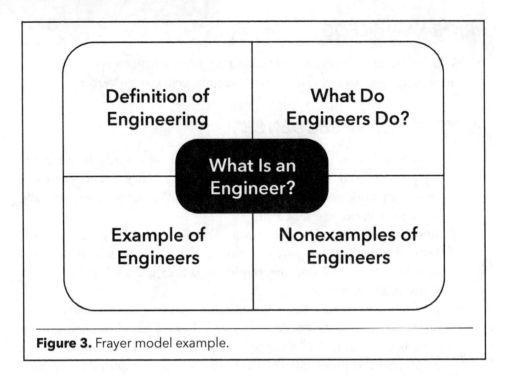

Figure 3. Frayer model example.

12. Then, have students debate whether or not the nonexamples are correct. Students may mention that even though certain jobs are limited to engineering, all jobs require problem solving. They require workers to ask questions, imagine, plan, create, and improve solutions. Because students have not yet been formally instructed on the engineering design process, they may not use this specific language, but try to direct them toward this idea.

13. Based on information collected on the Frayer model, have students construct a definition of an engineer (e.g., "a person who uses scientific knowledge to ask and address complex problems and design and create solutions to those problem").

EXTENSION ACTIVITIES

• Conduct an engineering scavenger hunt. Have students hunt for items in the classroom that were engineered to solve problems. Students should list each item and the problem that the product solved.

• Have students work with a partner to brainstorm a problem that could be solved through engineering. Guide students to create a prototype or description of the solution.

ASSESSMENT OBSERVATIONS

- Students should provide a diverse representation of engineers solving problems and developing products in their engineer drawings.
- Students should use evidence when debating examples and nonexamples. Students should clarify and support their choices.
- Students should begin connecting problem solving to a set of sequential but cyclic steps similar to the engineering design process. They should connect this to work of engineers and to their own problem solving.

LESSON 1.1

Draw an Engineer Test[1]

Directions: In the space below, draw a picture of an engineer at work. Then answer the prompts that follow.

```


```

Describe your picture.

1 Adapted from NASA and Design Squad, 2008. Copyright 2008 by NASA and Design Squad. Adapted with permission.

Thinking Like an Engineer © Taylor & Francis.

NAME: _____ DATE: _____

Draw an Engineer Test, continued

Compare your drawing to your group members' drawings. Using checkmarks, indicate which characteristics each group member included in his or her drawing.

Characteristics of an Engineer

	Picture of a male engineer	Picture of a female engineer	White coat	Tools	Auto-mobiles	Building	Hard hat	Images of products of engineering
Student 1:								
Student 2:								
Student 3:								
Student 4:								

LESSON 1.2

THINK LIKE AN ENGINEER

RESOURCES AND MATERIALS

- Lesson 1.2 Book Study
- Lesson 1.2 Habits of Mind
- *Whoosh!: Lonnie Johnson's Super-Soaking Stream of Inventions* by Chris Barton (student copies or class copy)

ESTIMATED TIME

45 minutes

OBJECTIVES

In this lesson, students will:
- identify characteristics and habits of mind of good problem solvers and engineers,
- self-assess their habits of mind, and
- evaluate how engineers use habits of mind to solve problems.

CONTENT

The suggested biography is *Whoosh!: Lonnie Johnson's Super-Soaking Stream of Inventions* by Chris Barton. However, you may find a different biography more suitable for your location and students. The students should be presented with a list of questions that examine challenges and characteristics of the engineer in solving problems (See Lesson 1.2 Book Study).

PRIOR KNOWLEDGE

Skills: group work and collaboration
Vocabulary: characteristics, personality, challenges, habits of mind

INSTRUCTIONAL SEQUENCE

1. Have students read *Whoosh!: Lonnie Johnson's Super-Soaking Stream of Inventions.* The reading can be done as a whole group, in small groups, or individually.
2. Before, during, or after reading the book, present the questions from Lesson 1.2 Book Study. Have students complete the handout individually, or consider the following options for student responses:
   - Divide students into groups of 2–3 and have them discuss these questions with each other. They can record their group answers and share question 7 with the class.
   - Have students individually answer questions 1–6. Students can then answer question 7 in a whole-group discussion (brainstorming).
   - Use an app or website, such as Google Classroom, Seesaw, Flipgrid, Poll Everywhere, or Socrative, to elicit and share student responses.
   - Divide the questions into sections: Before Reading (questions 1–3), During Reading (question 4), and After Reading (questions 5–7). Have students answer the questions at the appropriate stage of the reading process.

3. Give each student a copy of Lesson 1.2 Habits of Mind to complete. You may need to discuss each habit of mind as students fill in the chart.
4. Divide students into groups of 3–4. Students should discuss which habit of mind is most important for engineers. Have groups share with the class, using evidence to support their answers. For example, if a group chose "Taking Responsible Risks" as the most important habit of mind, students might discuss how many things are learned through mistakes or accidents, such as Lonnie making the Super Soaker. Alternatively, this step could be an individual assignment (e.g., a student reflection) if preferred.

EXTENSION ACTIVITY

Have students research things that were created by accident or mistake. Alexander Fleming's discovery of penicillin is a good example (see https://www.storypick.com/inventions-made-by-mistake). Other accidental inventions can be found at https://www.brainjet.com/random/2353130/15-everyday-items-that-were-invented-by-accident.

ASSESSMENT OBSERVATIONS

- As students read *Whoosh!: Lonnie Johnson's Super-Soaking Stream of Inventions*, they should recognize that Lonnie is curious, persistent, and driven. Students should see these characteristics in themselves as they address challenges they face in their own lives.
- Students should recognize that all habits of mind are necessary for engineers and problem solvers.
- Students should recognize how they can improve their habits of mind and how they use them in solving problems.

LESSON 1.2
Book Study

Directions: Answer the following questions, considering what you learned in *Whoosh!: Lonnie Johnson's Super-Soaking Stream of Inventions*.

1. Describe a challenge that you face every day. How do you work to overcome that challenge?

2. What do you love to do?

3. Have you ever been told you could not do something, but you knew you could? What did you do?

4. What are some characteristics or personality traits that make Lonnie a good problem solver and a good engineer?

5. When facing challenges, what characteristics do you have that help you with the challenge?

6. How do your characteristics compare with Lonnie's?

7. What characteristics do you think engineers need to have to solve problems?

NAME: _____ DATE: _____

LESSON 1.2
Habits of Mind

Directions: Complete the following chart. In the "Lonnie's Habits" column, place a checkmark by the habits of mind that Lonnie demonstrated. In the "My Habits" column, place a checkmark by habits of mind you demonstrate and an "x" by the habits of mind that need improvement.

Habit of Mind	What Does This Look Like?	Lonnie's Habits	My Habits
Persistence			
Managing Impulsivity			
Listening With Understanding and Empathy			
Thinking Flexibly			
Thinking About Thinking			
Striving for Accuracy			
Questioning and Posing Problems			
Applying Knowledge to New Situations			
Thinking and Communicating With Clarity and Precision			

Habits of Mind, continued

Habit of Mind	What Does This Look Like?	Lonnie's Habits	My Habits
Gathering Data Through All Senses			
Creating, Imagining, Innovating			
Responding With Wonderment and Awe			
Taking Responsible Risks			
Finding Humor			
Thinking Interdependently			
Remaining Open to Continuous Learning			

Which habits of mind you think engineers use the most?

LESSON 1.3

EXPLORE LIKE AN ENGINEER

RESOURCES AND MATERIALS

- Lesson 1.3 Index Card Tower
- Lesson 1.3 Reflection
- 50 notecards (per group of 3–4 students)
- Cell phone or other "load"

ESTIMATED TIME

75 minutes

OBJECTIVES

In this lesson, students will:
- work together to solve a problem and create a design for the solution,
- discuss the benefits of having time to brainstorm solutions and improve their designs, and
- explain the steps of the engineering design process and apply it to problem-solving activities.

CONTENT

During the engineering design process, many students jump to the Create stage before the Plan stage. This lesson should help students recognize the need for planning. Using a constructivist approach, students can experience the activity before understanding the purpose of a project. This allows for more meaningful learning by giving students context for new information.

PRIOR KNOWLEDGE

Skills: collaboration
Vocabulary: force, load, stable, unstable, geometric shapes, engineering design process

INSTRUCTIONAL SEQUENCE

1. Place students in groups of 3–4 and distribute a copy of Lesson 1.3 Index Card Tower to each group. Tell students: *Your challenge is to build the tallest tower you can with only 50 index cards.*
2. Distribute 50 notecards per group. Allow students 15 minutes (adjust as needed) to complete the task.
3. After the time has expired, instruct students to measure the height of their tower and conduct the "cell phone test." The tower must be able to support a cell phone (or other load) for at least 60 seconds.
4. Ask students to explain the process they used to construct their towers. Introduce students to the engineering design process (see Figure 1 in the Introduction). Explain and discuss the five steps: Ask, Imagine, Plan, Create, and Improve. Ask students:
   - What are the benefits of each step?
   - How does each step contribute to the process?
   - What happens when an engineer completes the Improve stage?
   - Are the steps always the same? Are they always completed in order?

5. Distribute Lesson 1.3 Reflection. Ask students to reflect on how they could improve their tower.

EXTENSION ACTIVITY

Conduct an augmented reality (AR) activity using an app such as HP Reveal. Have students create an AR trigger with the picture of their tower. They can embed a video behind the tower explaining the steps of the engineering design process. For example, using a poster of the engineering design process, one group could focus on the first step of the engineering design process. That group could use the Ask emblem as their trigger in HP Reveal and embed their created video in that emblem; when students scan the Ask emblem using the app, the video would play.

Note. HP Reveal is a useful app at the time of this book's printing. Feel free to adapt this activity using another relevant application.

ASSESSMENT OBSERVATIONS

- Students should work in a group to create a solution to the problem.
- Students should recognize the benefits of the engineering design process in solving problems.
- Students should list the steps of the engineering design process but recognize that the process is cyclical and the steps could vary.

LESSON 1.3

Index Card Tower

Challenge

Build the tallest tower that can support a cell phone, using only 50 index cards.

Criteria

- The tower must support a load (cell phone) for at least 60 seconds.
- The tower must be freestanding; it cannot be attached to the table or ceiling.

Constraints

- You must use all 50 index cards.
- You have 15 minutes to complete the task.

LESSON 1.3

Reflection

Directions: Reflect on the engineering design process you used to create your index card tower. Consider what worked and what could be improved.

1. What did you do to ensure you were addressing the requirements of the tower?

2. How did you determine what design you were going to use?

3. If you were to do this activity again, what would you want to do differently?

4. How did you follow the engineering design process?

UNIT 2
WHO CAN BE AN ENGINEER?

RATIONALE

This unit will provide students with opportunities to learn about the branches of engineering and the steps they might take to become engineers. Students should also have the opportunity to meet and interact with professional engineers, either in person or virtually.

PLAN

In Lesson 2.1, students will utilize various resources to learn about engineers and their jobs. They will read articles, explore websites, and examine different types of engineering fields. In Lesson 2.2, students will participate in virtual field trips and connect to practicing engineers through virtual and face-to-face formats. In Lesson 2.3, students will create a job description for an engineering field of interest to them.

LESSON 2.1

WHAT ARE THE TYPES OF ENGINEERS?

RESOURCES AND MATERIALS

- Lesson 2.1 Engineering Career Resources
- Lesson 2.1 Engineering Branch Summary Table
- Lesson 2.1 What Kind of Engineer Should I Be?
- Student computers or tablets with Internet access

ESTIMATED TIME

45–60 minutes

OBJECTIVES

In this lesson, students will:
- compare and contrast the roles of engineers in various branches,
- describe engineering branches and their contributions to society, and
- distinguish between the career path of engineers in various branches.

CONTENT

This lesson will focus on the various branches of engineering. Students will examine multiple resources and distinguish between the roles engineers have in the various branches of engineering. Students will complete a table comparing and contrasting branches of engineering by their purpose, job roles, contributions to society, and career path.

PRIOR KNOWLEDGE

Skills: compare and contrast, group work, and research using websites and videos

Vocabulary: purpose, job roles, contribution, society, career

INSTRUCTIONAL SEQUENCE

1. Divide students into small groups of 2–3. Students may select an engineering field of interest, or you may assign each group an engineering field.
2. Instruct groups to utilize the provided resources (see Lesson 2.1 Engineering Career Resources) to determine the purpose, job roles, contribution to society, and career path of their assigned branch of engineering. Each group should record their information using Lesson 2.1 Engineering Branch Summary Table. *Note.* Contributions to society can be specific, such as landmarks (e.g., Golden Gate Bridge), or general (e.g., transportation systems). You could also ask students to find both an example of a general contribution and a more specific contribution.
3. Have all groups share their information with the other groups until the students have completed their tables for all branches of engineering. You may have students orally present or work with several partners until they have all of the necessary information.
4. Other branches of engineering can be added to the table as needed.
5. Students should keep this information to be used throughout Unit 2.

EXTENSION ACTIVITY

Distribute Lesson 2.1 What Kind of Engineer Should I Be? Students should consider the pros and cons of a few engineering branches, and then select their favorite branch.

ASSESSMENT OBSERVATIONS

- Students should be able to distinguish between the branches by their main purpose (e.g., "Biomedical engineers solve problems related to the body and medicine, and aerospace engineers solve problems related to air and space travel").
- Students should evaluate the various contributions of engineers to society (general and/or specific).
- Students should identify how engineers typically focus on math and science in high school and university studies.

NAME: _____ DATE: _____

LESSON 2.1
Engineering Career Resources

The following videos, articles, and resources are helpful places to begin when exploring different engineering careers.

Videos

Type of Engineer	Video	Link
Civil Engineer	"Career Spotlight: Civil Engineer" by KQED Quest	https://www.youtube.com/watch?v=t8nvuASMdhU
	"What Do Civil Engineers Do?" by American Society of Civil Engineers	https://www.youtube.com/watch?v=cJaRjl7K-Lw
Electrical Engineer	"What Is an Electrical Engineer?" by The MEProgram	https://www.youtube.com/watch?v=ujrEme2UoLM
Environmental Engineer	"Environmental Engineers – Careers in Science and Engineering" by National Science Foundation	https://www.youtube.com/watch?v=k2epvAUEdCl
	"Careers in STEM – Environmental Engineer Featuring Erin McGregor" by the Dow Chemical Company	https://www.youtube.com/watch?v=1e1ZiPjxUw4
Chemical Engineer	"Cool Careers: Chemical Engineer" by MindFuel Canada	https://www.youtube.com/watch?v=_UXwbxM8Yfl
Hardware Engineer	"Meet Hardware Engineers at Google" by Life at Google	https://www.youtube.com/watch?v=OdmSXXfknU8
Biomedical Engineer	"Tejal Desai, Biomedical Engineer" by UC San Francisco	https://www.youtube.com/watch?v=KSmQ3F21ovo
Mechanical Engineer	"Neena Gandhi: Mechanical Engineer" by Techsploration	https://www.youtube.com/watch?v=dGPP5rHn8ko
	"What Is Mechanical Engineering?" by Iowa State University College of Engineering	https://www.youtube.com/watch?v=IC862DXkLTA
Aeronautical Engineer	"Scientist Profile: Aeronautical Engineer" by PBS LearningMedia	https://pbslearningmedia.org/resource/4a2413ec-b0fc-4438-8545-80897653f793/4a2413ec-b0fc-4438-8545-80897653f793

Thinking Like an Engineer © Taylor & Francis.

NAME: _____ DATE: _____

Engineering Career Resources, continued

Articles

Type of Engineer	Article	Link
Civil Engineer	"Interview With Civil Engineer Don. S." by Audrey Stern	http://www.teenink.com/nonfiction/interviews/article/49652/Interview-with-Civil-Engineer-Don-S
	"A Day in the Life of a Civil Engineer" by The Princeton Review	https://www.princetonreview.com/careers/36/civil-engineer
Electrical Engineer	"Who Builds Big? Interview: Tiffany Ann Clute, P.E., Electrical Engineer" by PBS Online	http://www.pbs.org/wgbh/buildingbig/profile/interview/index.html
Environmental Engineer	"Interview With an Environmental Engineer" by Houghton Mifflin Harcourt	https://hmdecozine.com/careers/environmental-engineer
Chemical Engineer	"What Do Chemical Engineers Do?" by AIChE	https://www.aiche.org/community/students/career-resources-k-12-students-parents/what-do-chemical-engineers-do
	"Five Everyday Products and the Chemical Engineering That Goes Into Them (Day 148)" by Geoff Maitland	https://ichemeblog.org/2014/10/22/five-every-day-products-and-the-chemical-engineering-that-goes-into-them-day-148
Computer Engineer	"What is Computer Engineering?" by Jim Lucas	https://www.livescience.com/48326-computer-engineering.html
Biomedical Engineer	"What is Biomedical Engineering?" by Jim Lucas	https://www.livescience.com/48001-biomedical-engineering.html
	"Meet a Real Biomedical Engineer, Abby Vogel" by LifeWorks	http://nihlifeworks.org/Interviews/Abby%2bVogel.html
Mechanical Engineer	"A Kids Guide to Mechanics and Engineering" by Maddy Martin	https://www.yourmechanic.com/article/a-kid-s-guide-to-mechanics-and-engineering-by-maddy-martin
	"Profiles of Mechanical Engineers: Lori Laird" by American Society of Mechanical Engineers	http://tryengineering.org/sites/default/files/tryengineering_profile_14.pdf
Aerospace Engineer	"Careers in Aerospace Technology" by NASA	https://www.nasa.gov/centers/langley/news/factsheets/FS-2001-09-68-LaRC.html

General Resources

- Careers in Science by Science Buddies (https://www.sciencebuddies.org/science-engineering-careers#engineering)
- Engineer Girl (https://www.engineergirl.org)
- eGFI (http://www.egfi-k12.org)
- NASA for Educators (https://www.nasa.gov/audience/foreducators/index.html)

NAME: _____ DATE: _____

LESSON 2.1
Engineering Branch Summary Table

Directions: Research the purpose, job roles, contribution, and career path for your assigned branch of engineering. Then, fill out the rest of the table as the other groups present their findings.

Branch of Engineering	Purpose	Job Roles	Contribution	Career Path
Civil				
Mechanical				
Aerospace				
Computer				

Thinking Like an Engineer © Taylor & Francis.

NAME: _____ DATE: _____

Engineering Branch Summary Table, continued

Branch of Engineering	Purpose	Job Roles	Contribution	Career Path
Biomedical				
Electrical				
Environmental				
Chemical				
Other:				

LESSON 2.1
What Kind of Engineer Should I Be?

Directions: Imagine you are getting ready to graduate high school and pursue engineering in college. Select your two or three favorite branches and prepare a list of pros and cons for each branch. The pros and cons can include subjects and classes you would study in college, job roles, job demand, salary, etc.

Branch 1: _____

Pros	Cons

Branch 2: _____

Pros	Cons

Thinking Like an Engineer © Taylor & Francis.

What Kind of Engineer Should I Be?, continued

Branch 3: _____

Pros	Cons

What is your favorite branch of engineering. Why is it your favorite branch?

LESSON 2.2

MEET AN ENGINEER

RESOURCES AND MATERIALS

- Lesson 1.2 Habits of Mind
- Lesson 2.1 Engineering Branch Summary Table
- Lesson 2.2 Career Day Questions
- Career day contacts with local professional engineers or engineers found through programs such as Skype for Educators (https://education. microsoft.com/skype-in-the-classroom/find-guest-speakers)
- *Whoosh!: Lonnie Johnson's Super-Soaking Stream of Inventions* by Chris Barton (student copies or class copy)

ESTIMATED TIME

60 minutes to plan and 3 hours to conduct Career Day (time will vary depending on number of engineer visitors; allow on average 10–20 minutes for each speaker); 45 minutes for reflection

OBJECTIVES

In this lesson, students will:
- recognize roles engineers have in their jobs,
- identify common characteristics that help engineers become good problem solvers, and
- outline career paths of engineers from various branches.

CONTENT

This lesson will continue to focus on engineering as a career. Students will investigate the roles of engineers in their society; compare and contrast the knowledge, skills, and characteristics of engineers from various branches; and engage in virtual or face-to-face conversations with practicing engineers. Students should help organize a career day with engineers from various branches.

PRIOR KNOWLEDGE

Skills: group work, collaboration, communicating
Knowledge: habits of mind
Vocabulary: characteristics, challenges, engineering

INSTRUCTIONAL SEQUENCE

1. Organize a career day in which students will have opportunities to speak to engineers in the community. Involve students in the planning process by asking if they have parents, friends, or family in engineering careers. Students could then get in touch with those contacts and invite them to attend career day. Alternatively or in addition, you might arrange a virtual career day in which students connect with engineers through online platforms, such as Skype for Educators.

2. Prior to meeting with engineers, have students in groups of 2–3 develop a list of questions to ask the engineers (e.g., *What do you do in your typical day? How did you decide to become an engineer? What are some problems that you solved when you were a young student? What are some of your characteristics that make you a good engineer?*). Students may record their questions on Lesson 2.2 Career Day Questions. Students can revisit the book *Whoosh!: Lonnie Johnson's Super-Soaking Stream of Inventions* to help construct questions for the engineers. Students can see if Lonnie's experiences are similar to those of other engineers. For example, students might ask the engineers, "Did you enjoy inventing things when you were a young child?" or "Have you experienced failure as an engineer? How did you respond to that failure?"

3. Students should also seek information from the engineers on career day about career options and pathways, identifying problems to solve, finding new information to solve problems, and the engineering design process.

4. Conduct the career day. Students should come prepared with questions and take notes during the presentations.

5. After the career day, have students revisit Lesson 2.1 Engineering Branch Summary Table and Lesson 1.2 Habits of Mind. They can and add or modify the tables with new information they obtained from career day.

6. Have students write a thank-you note to each engineer who participated in the career day.

EXTENSION ACTIVITY

Have student develop a newspaper article about career day. Students should share the information they learned from the engineers with other classes throughout the school.

ASSESSMENT OBSERVATIONS

- Students should have questions prepared before career day.
- Students should recognize similar habits of mind and characteristics among the career day engineers, Lonnie from the book study, and themselves.
- Students should contribute to career day by suggesting parents, friends, or family that may be engineers, developing questions for the engineers, and contributing to the overall conversation with engineers.

LESSON 2.2
Career Day Questions

Directions: Below are prompts to help you develop questions for career day. You are not restricted to these prompts and can add additional questions approved by your teacher. Consider asking about the engineers' day-to-day work, their motivation, and their characteristics. Revisit *Whoosh!: Lonnie Johnson's Super-Soaking Stream of Inventions* to help you think about what engineers do and what you would like to know more about.

Childhood

Question 1:

Question 2:

School

Question 3:

Question 4:

College

Question 5:

Question 6:

Career Day Questions, continued

Adulthood

Question 7:

Question 8:

Characteristics of a Good Engineer

Question 9:

Question 10:

Job Roles

Question 11:

Question 12:

Thinking Like an Engineer © Taylor & Francis.

LESSON 2.3

CREATE A JOB DESCRIPTION

RESOURCES AND MATERIALS

- Lesson 2.3 Job Description
- Job-seeking websites
  - Indeed (https://www.indeed.com)
  - Monster (https://www.monster.com)
  - CareerBuilder (https://www.careerbuilder.com)
  - EngineerJobs.com (https://www.engineerjobs.com)

- Student computers with Google Docs, Word, Publisher, or Book Creator

ESTIMATED TIME

150 minutes

OBJECTIVES

In this lesson, students will:
- create a job description for an engineer in a specific branch of engineering, and
- share their job description using a preferred mode of presentation.

CONTENT

In this lesson, students use the information they have gathered throughout the unit and career day to create a job description for an engineer in their chosen or assigned branch. Students may work alone or in groups to achieve this task. Students will create a presentation of their choice (brochure, e-book, poster, etc.) to present the job description.

PRIOR KNOWLEDGE

Skills: computer presentation
Knowledge: engineer job requirements
Vocabulary: job description, salary, characteristics

INSTRUCTIONAL SEQUENCE

1. Instruct students to create a job description for a particular engineering job, using information obtained from the previous lesson. Facilitate students' review of the characteristics of engineers by revisiting the class Frayer model constructed in Lesson 1.1 and adding additional characteristics to the model as found in career day.

2. As a class, develop a list of engineering branches. Students should determine the engineering branch they will focus on for this activity. Students could complete the activity in groups based on their chosen branch.

3. Have students search job-seeking websites for engineering jobs and their requirements.

4. Distribute Lesson 2.3 Job Description. Students should assemble information for a job description for an engineering job in their chosen or assigned branch. Students can use a real or fictional company for the job description. Information they should gather includes:
   - a list of characteristics that engineers need,
   - education requirements,
   - job roles,
   - company name and purpose, and
   - starting and average salaries.

5. In their preferred mode of presentation, students or student groups will share the job description with the class. Students may choose to create a brochure, slideshow presentation, digital book, poster, etc. The presentation will be graded on the completeness and accuracy of the information. Additionally, students could complete a poll indicating which job they would want to take and why.

EXTENSION ACTIVITES

- Have students compose a mock letter to a company that is advertising an engineering job opening. Have students pretend they have just completed their degree and are ready to enter the workforce as an engineer. The letter should include information about their education, experience in engineering, and their characteristics that make them a qualified candidate. The company could be from their created job description, another students' created job description, or another company they found in the advertisements.
- Students could conduct and participate in mock job interviews for their advertised job.

ASSESSMENT OBSERVATION

Students should use the characteristics and skills of engineers that have been discussed in previous lessons when creating their job descriptions.

LESSON 2.3
Job Description

Directions: Research your chosen or assigned engineering branch using a job-seeking website. You will be writing and presenting a job description using the following information.

1. What is the company's name and purpose?

2. What does the job role entail?

3. What characteristics does an engineer need to succeed in this job?

4. What education requirements must an engineer meet for this job?

5. What is the starting salary for this role?

6. What is the average salary for engineers at this company?

UNIT 3
DESIGN CITIES LIKE AN ENGINEER

RATIONALE

In this unit, students will solve real-world problems in relation to designing a city. Students will complete challenges in civil, electrical, and mechanical engineering. Each design challenge provides a problem scenario, challenge, constraints, criteria, and materials representative of the theme. You may elect to do each challenge in the unit, select particular challenges for the class to complete, or allow groups of students to choose which challenge they would like to do. This is an opportunity for students to solve problems like engineers.

PLAN

In Lesson 3.1, students will act as civil engineers and be provided a real-world problem scenario to design and create a skyscraper to maximize space in a large, crowded city. In Lesson 3.2, students will act as electrical engineers and be challenged to add working lights to the skyscraper created in Lesson 3.1. In Lesson 3.3, students will act as mechanical engineers in designing and creating a Ferris wheel to go in the city park.

Note. The engineering journal included with Lesson 3.1 may be used to apply the engineering design process to any of the challenges in Units 3–5.

LESSON 3.1
CIVIL ENGINEER CHALLENGE

RESOURCES AND MATERIALS

- Lesson 3.1 Amazon Skyscraper
- Lesson 3.1 My Engineering Journal
- Building materials (per group):
  - 100 toothpicks
  - 50 gumdrops
  - Measuring tape
  - Blow dryer or fan

- Web resources:
  - "Motion Basics" by Physics4Kids.com (http://www.physics4kids.com/files/motion_intro.html)
  - "Physics for Kids" by Ducksters (https://www.ducksters.com/science/physics/force.php)
  - "Shapes That Make Structures Strong" by PBS LearningMedia (https://www.pbslearningmedia.org/resource/phy03.sci.phys.mfw.lp_shapes/shapes-that-make-structures-strong)

ESTIMATED TIME

3–4 hours

OBJECTIVES

In this lesson, students will:
- collaborate to solve a civil engineering problem,
- create a design and prototype for the solution, and
- determine the footprint of a building by applying appropriate calculations.

CONTENT

In this lesson, students will act as civil engineers by submitting a proposal to build a new Amazon building in their city. The lesson should follow the sequence of Ask, Imagine, Plan, Create, and Improve.

PRIOR KNOWLEDGE

Skills: collaboration, group work

Knowledge: Calculations using multiplication, division, ratios, and perimeter; forces; gravity; wind speed

Vocabulary: force, gravity, perimeter, structure, infrastructure, prototype or model, footprint

INSTRUCTIONAL SEQUENCE

1. **Ask:**
   - Place students in groups of 3–4 and distribute Lesson 3.1 Amazon Skyscraper. Present the problem: *You are a civil engineer in _____, where there is a shortage of space for any new buildings. In a recent competition by Amazon, your city was selected as the new location for Amazon headquarters. In the promise to Amazon, the city agreed to build a new skyscraper—the largest in the city. However, there is very little land available for a new building. In order to accommodate Amazon, the skyscraper will need to be taller than any building in the city. There are many other issues to consider including stability of the tower.* Make the challenge specific to your city or location. For example, you might have students specify the name of your city or a nearby large metropolitan city.
   - Have students begin working on Lesson 3.1 My Engineering Journal, which is divided into the steps of the engineering design process (this handout can also be used for all other challenges in Units 3–5). Groups should complete a Need to Know Chart in the Ask section of Lesson 3.1 My Engineering Journal, indicating what they know from reading the scenario, what they need to know to help solve the problem, and what they need to do. Students should include the criteria and constraints of the challenge in the "know" portion of the chart. (*Note.* You may use another type of graphic organizer if desired.)
   - As a class, discuss types of shapes that are stable, the kinds of forces that act on buildings, and gravity, using web resources as necessary (see Resources and Materials).

2. **Imagine:**
   - Have student groups revisit the Need to Know chart and add information as needed.

- Student groups should brainstorm ideas for the tallest building with the smallest footprint that is still stable. Students should agree upon the best solution or plan to complete the challenge.

3. **Plan:**
   - Have student groups develop a plan to create a prototype of the building.
   - Student groups should construct a diagram and label all parts of the building. They should also develop a list of materials needed to complete their prototype or test. (You may provide students with a list of materials available for use.)

4. **Create:**
   - Student groups will follow their plans to construct the prototype of the building. You may want to give a time limit (30 minutes) and adjust as needed.
   - Student groups should measure the height of their building and the perimeter of their building, recording their results on Lesson 3.1 Amazon Skyscraper Challenge. The perimeter is the distance around the base or the sum of the sides. Students will then calculate the ratio of the height to perimeter—H:P or H/P.
   - Have student groups conduct stability tests to see if their buildings can remain standing in windy conditions. The building should be placed one meter away from the blow dryer or fan. Have students test to see if it remains standing at different wind speeds and record their results on Lesson 3.1 Amazon Skyscraper. You may adjust the distance as needed or have students test at several distances.

5. **Improve:**
   - Have students reflect on the Improve questions from Lesson 3.1 My Engineering Journal.
   - Allow students time to improve their design and to retest. Students should take a picture or complete a drawing of their building and add it to their journals.

EXTENSION ACTIVITIES

- Have students sketch the tower and indicate all of the forces that are acting on the tower. Students should use Newton's first law to describe how the tower remained standing and why it fell.
- Ask students to use an online map maker (e.g., Animap) to create a map that represents the location and city where the new Amazon building is located.
- Student groups could prepare a presentation of the proposal to convince Amazon to use their plan for the building. The presentation could be in the form of a video, brochure, e-book, etc.

ASSESSMENT OBSERVATIONS

- Students should work in a group to create a solution to the problem.
- Students should recognize the benefits of the engineering design process in solving problems.
- Students should be able to determine the footprint of the tower by applying appropriate calculations. If the base of the tower is an irregular shape, instruct students to adjust the measurements to reflect the appropriate shape.

NAME: _____   DATE: _____

LESSON 3.1
Amazon Skyscraper

Problem/Challenge

You are a civil engineer in _____, where there is a shortage of space for any new buildings. In a recent competition by Amazon, your city was selected as the new location for Amazon headquarters. In the promise to Amazon, your city agreed to build a new skyscraper—the largest in the city. However, there is very little land available for a new building. In order to accommodate Amazon, the skyscraper will need to be taller than any building in the city. There are many other issues to consider, including the stability of the tower.

Materials

- 100 toothpicks
- 50 gumdrops
- Measuring tape
- Blow dryer or fan

Criteria

- The skyscraper should be as tall as possible with the smallest perimeter to minimize its footprint in the city.
- The skyscraper must be able to withstand wind gusts without falling over.

Constraints

- You must only use the materials provided.
- The skyscraper must be freestanding and not taped/attached to the desk or to anything else.

Ratio Table

Directions: Record the height of your tower, the perimeter of the base of your tower, and the ratio of the height to the perimeter.

Height (cm)	Perimeter (cm)	Ratio

48

Thinking Like an Engineer © Taylor & Francis.

Amazon Skyscraper, continued

Stability Test

Directions: Indicate with a Y or N if your tower remained standing after each wind speed (Y = Tower still standing; N = Tower fell down). You may also test the effect of the wind speed at different distances.

Distance	Low Wind Speed	Medium Wind Speed	High Wind Speed
1 meter			

LESSON 3.1

My Engineering Journal

Directions: Complete the questions in this engineering journal to explore the engineering design process pictured below.

Adapted from Engineering is Elementary, 2018.

Thinking Like an Engineer © Taylor & Francis.

My Engineering Journal, continued

Step 1: Ask

1. What is the problem you are trying to solve?

2. What has been done to solve this problem before?

3. What are the criteria and constraints?

4. What materials are available?

5. Need to Know Chart

What I Know	What I Need to Know	How Do I Find Out?

My Engineering Journal, continued

Step 2: Imagine

How do you plan on solving the problem? Brainstorm with your group to come up with many possible solutions. Choose the best idea or combine ideas to form a new idea, using the organizer below.

	Will this help the problem or meet the challenge?	Do we have the materials to do this?	Is this easy to do?	Number of "yes" responses.
Idea #1:				
Idea #2:				
Idea #3				
Idea #4				

Thinking Like an Engineer © Taylor & Francis.

My Engineering Journal, continued

Step 3: Plan

1. Diagram your plan below. Label all parts.

2. What materials will you need to build your prototype or design?

My Engineering Journal, continued

Step 4: Create

Create and test your design/prototype. Draw a picture or insert a picture of your completed design below.

My Engineering Journal, continued

Step 5: Improve

1. What worked well with your design?

2. What went wrong?

3. How could you make the design better?

LESSON 3.2

ELECTRICAL ENGINEER CHALLENGE

RESOURCES AND MATERIALS

- Lesson 3.1 My Engineering Journal
- Lesson 3.2 Light It Up
- Lesson 3.2 Circuits
- Lighting materials (per group of 3–4):
  - 10 miniature light bulbs (Christmas lights cut with about 2 inches of wire attached to the light work well)
  - 2 batteries
  - 2 battery holders
  - 5 wire connectors

- Web resources:
  - "Circuits" by DK (https://www.dkfindout.com/us/science/electricity/circuits)
  - "Science Games for Kids: Electricity Circuits" by Science Kids (http://www.sciencekids.co.nz/gamesactivities/electricitycircuits.html)
  - "Lesson: Get Charged! Introduction to Electrical Energy" by Teach-Engineering (https://www.teachengineering.org/lessons/view/cub_energy2_lesson04)

ESTIMATED TIME

3–4 hours

OBJECTIVES

In this lesson, students will:
- collaborate to solve an electrical engineering problem,
- construct a circuit with a battery and miniature lights, and
- explain the path of a current (i.e., open and closed circuits, as well as series and parallel circuits).

CONTENT

In this lesson, students will work as electrical engineers. This is a continuation of the Amazon challenge, but this time students will be acting as electrical engineers. The lesson should follow the sequence of Ask, Imagine, Plan, Create, and Improve.

PRIOR KNOWLEDGE

Skills: collaboration, group work, data collection
Knowledge: simple and parallel circuits, DC and AC power, alternative energy sources
Vocabulary: electricity, circuits, series and parallel circuits, current, power source

INSTRUCTIONAL SEQUENCE

1. **Ask:**
   - Place students in groups of 3–4 and distribute Lesson 3.2 Light It Up. Explain: *You are an electrical engineer in _____, where a new skyscraper has been built for Amazon's headquarters. The Federal Aviation Administration is concerned about the visibility of the building at night for air traffic. Your job is to add lights powered by direct current (battery) to the building.*
   - Students should complete a Need to Know Chart (in the Ask section of Lesson 3.1 My Engineering Journal) indicating what they know from reading the scenario, what they need to know to help solve the problem, and what they need to do. Students should include the criteria and constraints of the challenge in the "know" portion of the chart.
   - Discuss current, including AC and DC; alternative energy sources such as solar power; circuits; and the difference between series and parallel circuits. Distribute Lesson 3.2 Circuits for reference. See Resources and Materials for helpful web resources.

2. **Imagine:**
   - Have students revisit the Need to Know chart and add information as needed.

- Have student groups brainstorm ideas for the best way to add the most lights to the outside of the building. Students should agree upon the best solution or plan to complete the challenge.

3. **Plan:**
   - Have student groups develop a plan to create a lighted circuit for the outside of the building.
   - Student groups should construct a diagram and label all parts of the circuit. They should also develop a list of materials needed to complete their circuit. (You may provide students with a list of materials available for use.)

4. **Create:**
   - Student groups will follow their plans to add lights to the building. You may want to give a time limit (30 minutes) and adjust as needed.
   - Student groups should add at least four lights, and their structure should stay alight for at least 10 minutes. If students achieve this challenge, they should try to add more lights to the circuit.
   - If students created a series circuit (the simplest option), they should then attempt a parallel circuit.

5. **Improve:**
   - Have students reflect on the Improve questions in Lesson 3.1 My Engineering Journal.
   - Allow students time to improve their design and to retest. Students should take a picture or complete a drawing of their lighted building and add it to their journals.

EXTENSION ACTIVITY

Ask students to experiment with using different energy sources for their lights, such as solar power. For resources about alternate energy sources, see "Hands-on Activity: Potato Power" (https://www.teachengineering.org/activities/view/cub_energy2_lesson04_activity2) or "Hands-on Activity: Design a Solar City" (https://www.teachengineering.org/activities/view/cub_solarcity_activity1) by TeachEngineering.

ASSESSMENT OBSERVATIONS

- Students should work in a group to create a solution to the problem.
- Students should recognize the benefits of the engineering design process in solving problems.
- Students should be able to explain the difference between open and closed circuits and series and parallel circuits.

LESSON 3.2
Light It Up

Problem/Challenge

You are an electrical engineer in _____, where a new skyscraper has been built for Amazon's headquarters. The Federal Aviation Administration is concerned about the visibility of the tower at night for air traffic. Your job is to add lights powered by direct current (battery) to the tower.

Materials

- 10 miniature light bulbs
- 2 batteries
- 2 battery holders
- 5 wire connectors

Criteria

- The tower must include a minimum of four lights.
- The lights must shine for a minimum of 10 minutes.

Constraints

- You have 60 minutes to complete the project.
- Use only the available materials.

LESSON 3.2

Circuits

A circuit is a complete path in which electrical current can flow. It begins with a power source, such as a battery. The electrical current moves from one end of the battery to the other through wires. If the path is complete, current can flow. If it is not complete (i.e., if there is a break in the loop), current will not flow.

Lights in the path are known as resistors. When the current encounters a resistor, the resistor gets hot and the filament in the light will glow.

There are two types of circuits: series and parallel. Series circuits are how Christmas tree lights used to be made; when one light went out, all of the others went out. In parallel circuits, the current is able to bypass the burned-out light and still complete the circuit.

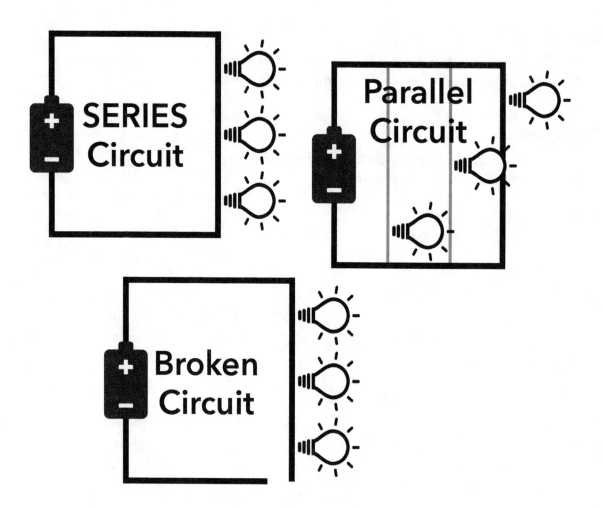

Thinking Like an Engineer © Taylor & Francis.

LESSON 3.3

MECHANICAL ENGINEER CHALLENGE

RESOURCES AND MATERIALS

- Lesson 3.1 My Engineering Journal
- Lesson 3.3 Design a Ferris Wheel
- Hair dryer or fan
- Materials for the Ferris wheel and brake: plastic plates, plastic cups, water bottle, pennies, tape, string, blow dryer, rulers, pencils, craft sticks, etc.
- Web resources:
  - "Simple Machines Game" by BrainPOP (https://www.brainpop.com/games/simplemachinesgame)
  - "Wheel and Axle" by Easy Science for Kids (https://easyscienceforkids.com/kids-the-wheel-and-axle)

ESTIMATED TIME

3–4 hours

OBJECTIVES

In this lesson, students will:
- collaborate to solve a mechanical engineering problem,
- design and create a wind-powered Ferris wheel with a brake, and
- identify items that have a wheel and axle.

CONTENT

In this lesson, students will work as mechanical engineers to design a wind-powered Ferris wheel. The lesson should follow the sequence of Ask, Imagine, Plan, Create, and Improve.

PRIOR KNOWLEDGE

Skills: collaboration, group work, data collection
Knowledge: force, gravity, wheel and axle, simple machines
Vocabulary: direction, motor, mechanics, force, velocity, speed, acceleration, motion, gravity, wheel and axle; centripetal Force; centripetal acceleration

INSTRUCTIONAL SEQUENCE

1. **Ask:**
   - Place students in groups of 3–4 and distribute Lesson 3.3 Design a Ferris Wheel. Present the problem: *An area in _____, where you work, is building an amusement park. As a mechanical engineer, you have been hired to design the Ferris wheel. To conserve energy, the Ferris wheel should be powered by wind. You will also need to add a break system to safely stop the Ferris wheel in case of emergency. You will add a figurine (about the size of an army man toy or a LEGO) to the seat of the Ferris wheel. You can make a seat belt with string. Using the available materials, design and create a Ferris wheel that will turn with the wind (hair dryer or fan) and can be mechanically stopped.*
   - Groups should complete a Need to Know Chart (in the Ask section of Lesson 3.1 My Engineering Journal) indicating what they know from reading the scenario, what they need to know to help solve the problem, and what they need to do. Students should include the criteria and constraints of the challenge in the "know" portion of the chart.
   - As a class, discuss simple machines and their function in making work easier. Guide students to consider the purpose of wheels and list a number of things in the classroom that use wheels. See Resources and Materials for helpful web resources.

2. **Imagine:**
   - Have student groups revisit the Need to Know chart and add information as needed.
   - Have student groups brainstorm ideas for the best way to design their Ferris wheel to meet the criteria. Students should agree upon the best solution or plan to complete the challenge.

3. **Plan:**
   - Have students develop a plan to design the Ferris wheel that addresses the criteria.
   - Student groups should construct a diagram of the Ferris wheel that includes seats and a seatbelt. They should also develop a list of materials needed to complete their prototype or test. (You may provide students with a list of materials available for use.)

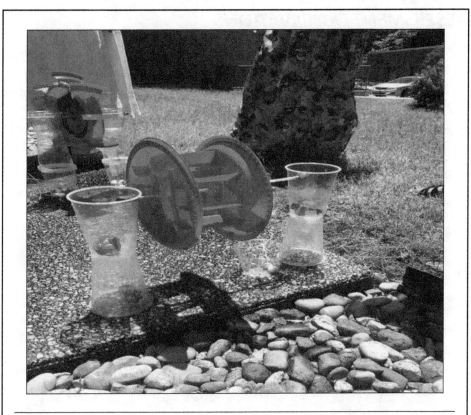

Figure 4. Ferris wheel examples.

4. **Create:**
   - Student groups will follow their plans to create the Ferris wheel. You may want to give a time limit (30 minutes) and adjust as needed.
   - Monitor students' progress and offer guidance as needed. See Figure 4 for examples of Ferris wheels constructed in the classroom.

5. **Improve:**
   - Have students reflect on the Improve questions from Lesson 3.1 My Engineering Journal.
   - Allow students time to improve their design to better meet the criteria.

EXTENSION ACTIVITIES

- Have students design a Ferris wheel on a digital fabrication site, such as Tinkercad (https://www.tinkercad.com). After designing the Ferris wheel, students could print using a 3-D printer.
- Advanced mathematics students could measure the angular velocity of the Ferris wheel. Help direct them to appropriate resources to learn about angular velocity.
- Extend learning by having students investigate centripetal force and acceleration.
- Conduct a book study on *Mr. Ferris and His Wheel* by Kathryn Gibbs Davis.

ASSESSMENT OBSERVATIONS

- Students should work together in a group to create a solution to the problem.
- Students should recognize the benefits of the engineering design process in solving problems.
- Students should recognize that wheels are used in many items to help make work easier.

LESSON 3.3
Design a Ferris Wheel

Problem/Challenge

An area in _____, where you work, is building an amusement park. As a mechanical engineer, you have been hired to design the Ferris wheel. To conserve energy, the Ferris wheel should be powered by wind. You will also need to add a break system to safely stop the Ferris wheel in case of emergency. You will add a figurine (about the size of an army man toy or a LEGO) to the seat of the Ferris wheel. You can also make a seatbelt with string. Using the available materials, design and create a Ferris wheel that will turn with the wind (hair dryer or fan) and can be mechanically stopped.

Materials

- Materials for the wheel and brake: plastic plates, plastic cups, water bottle, pennies, tape, string, rulers, pencils, craft sticks, etc.
- Blow dryer

Criteria

- The Ferris wheel should include seats and a brake to stop the motion.
- The passenger (figurine) must remain in the seat during the ride.

Constraints

- You must use the available materials.
- Your teacher will specify any other constraints.

Trial Run

Directions: Test your Ferris wheel, indicating its performance with a Y or N.
- Y = Ferris wheel turns, and passenger remains seated.
- N = Ferris wheel doesn't turn, or passenger doesn't remain seated.

Distance	Low Wind Speed	Medium Wind Speed	High Wind Speed
½ meter			

UNIT 4
CARE FOR YOUR WORLD LIKE AN ENGINEER

RATIONALE

In this unit, students will solve real-world problems in relation to caring for their world. Students will complete challenges in environmental, chemical, and biomedical engineering. Each design challenge provides a problem scenario, challenge, constraints, criteria, and materials representative of the theme. You may elect to do each challenge in the unit, select particular challenges for the class to complete, or allow groups of students to choose which challenge they would like to do. This is an opportunity for students to solve problems like engineers.

PLAN

In Lesson 4.1, students will act as environmental engineers and be provided a real-world problem scenario to improve water access for a country in need, such as Haiti. In Lesson 4.2, students will act as chemical engineers and be challenged to develop insecticides that are safe for the environment. In Lesson 3.3, students will act as biomedical engineers in designing and creating a working prosthetic hand for someone in need.

LESSON 4.1

ENVIRONMENTAL ENGINEER CHALLENGE

RESOURCES AND MATERIALS

- Lesson 3.1 My Engineering Journal
- Lesson 4.1 Water for Haiti
- Pipeline materials (per group):
  - 20 straws
  - 10 cups (marked with a water-level line)
  - 20 craft sticks
  - Clay
  - Tape

ESTIMATED TIME

3–4 hours

OBJECTIVES

In this lesson, students will:
- collaborate to plan, create, and test a water pipeline;
- calculate the efficiency of the water transportation system; and
- improve the water transportation system to increase its efficiency.

CONTENT

In this lesson, students will act as environmental engineers. Students will be working to improve water access for people in Haiti. The lesson should follow the sequence of Ask, Imagine, Plan, Create, and Improve.

PRIOR KNOWLEDGE

Skills: collaboration, group work, data collection

Knowledge: renewable resources, calculation of efficiency, human impact, measurement of liquids

Vocabulary: environment, habitat, ecosystem, human impact, renewable and nonrenewable resources

INSTRUCTIONAL SEQUENCE

1. **Ask:**
   - Place students in groups of 3–4 and distribute Lesson 4.1 Water for Haiti. Present the problem: *You are working as an environmental engineer in Haiti. The people of Haiti are in need of water transportation from a fresh spring to their villages. You will need to build a pipeline that travels 3 horizontal feet from the spring to the village.*
   - Groups should complete a Need to Know Chart (in the Ask section of Lesson 3.1 My Engineering Journal) indicating what they know from reading the scenario, what they need to know to help solve the problem, and what they need to do. Students should include the criteria and constraints of the challenge in the "know" portion of the chart.
   - As a class, discuss environmental and societal issues in high-poverty areas such as Haiti, the impact of humans on the environment, and how to calculate percentage of water collected (Percent of Collected Water = Beginning Amount ÷ Ending Amount x 100).

2. **Imagine:**
   - Have student groups revisit the Need to Know chart and add information as needed.
   - Have student groups brainstorm ideas for the best way to build the pipeline. Students should agree upon the best solution or plan to complete the challenge.

3. **Plan:**
   - Have student groups develop a plan to create a pipeline that addresses the criteria.
   - Student groups should construct a diagram and label all parts of the pipeline. They should also develop a list of materials needed to complete their pipeline. (You may provide students with a list of materials available for use.)

4. **Create:**
   - Student groups will follow their plans to create the pipeline. You may want to give a time limit (45 minutes) and adjust as needed.
   - Students will test their pipelines and determine the efficiency of the pipeline by determining the percent of transported water.
   - If pipelines lose too much water, groups should revisit their plan.

5. **Improve:**
   - Have students reflect on the Improve questions from Lesson 3.1 My Engineering Journal.
   - Allow students time to improve their design and to retest. Students should take a picture or complete a drawing of their pipeline and add it to their engineering journal.

EXTENSION ACTIVITY

Students could design and create a model of a system to clean water or to convert saltwater to freshwater. Resources include the following.

- "Clean Water Activity" by NASA (https://www.nasa.gov/audience/foreducators/topnav/materials/listbytype/Cleaning_Water_Activity.html)
- "Turn Salt Water Into Drinking Water" by Education.com (https://www.education.com/activity/article/Take_salt_out_of_salt_water)

ASSESSMENT OBSERVATIONS

- Students should work in a group to create a solution to the problem.
- Students should recognize the benefits of the engineering design process in solving problems.
- Students should revisit their design if the pipeline loses water.

LESSON 4.1
Water for Haiti

Problem/Challenge

You are working as an environmental engineer in Haiti. The people of Haiti are in need of water transportation from a fresh spring to their villages. You will need to build a pipeline that travels 3 horizontal feet from the spring to the village.

Materials

- 20 straws
- 10 plastic cups
- 20 craft sticks
- Clay
- Tape

Criteria

- The pipeline must fill an empty cup to the leveled line (marked by your teacher), and you can only add one cup of water to the pipeline.
- The pipeline must be above ground and not touch the flat surface at any time.
- The base of the pipeline must be 3 feet from the water source.

Constraints

- Use only the provided materials.
- The pipeline must be completed in 45 minutes.

Water Transportation Table

Directions: Measure the amount of water before and after you test your pipeline. Then calculate the percent of collected water.

Percent of Collected Water = Beginning Amount ÷ Ending Amount x 100

Beginning Amount of Water (mL)	Ending Amount of Water (mL)	Percent of Collected Water

LESSON 4.2

CHEMICAL ENGINEER CHALLENGE

RESOURCES AND MATERIALS

- Lesson 3.1 My Engineering Journal
- Lesson 4.2 Safe Insecticides
- Materials for experiment (per group of 3–4):
  - White paper
  - Paper cups
  - Cotton swabs
  - Small pieces of candy or fruit
  - Outside area with ant activity
  - Materials for solutions: water, sugar, lemon juice, vinegar, baking soda, dish soap, hand soap, hot pepper sauce, etc. (Note. Commercial ant repellents may be used if supervised by an adult.)

ESTIMATED TIME

3–4 hours

OBJECTIVES

In this lesson, students will:
- collaborate to solve a chemical engineering problem,
- create a design and prototype for the solution, and
- compare and contrast various ant repellents to determine the most effective one.

CONTENT

In this lesson, students will act as environmental engineers. Students will be working to develop a safe pesticide created from kitchen staples. The lesson should follow the sequence of Ask, Imagine, Plan, Create, and Improve.

PRIOR KNOWLEDGE

Skills: collaboration, group work, data collection, compare and contrast, construction of graphs

Knowledge: measurements, how to design a science experiment

Vocabulary: chemistry, reactions, chemical engineering, pesticide, repellent, acid, bases; attractants, control experiment, control, independent variable, dependent variable

INSTRUCTIONAL SEQUENCE

1. **Ask:**
   - Place students in groups of 3–4 and distribute Lesson 4.2 Safe Insecticides. Present the problem: *You are planning a big picnic at the park. During a recent visit, you noticed that ants were everywhere, including on the picnic tables. You do not want to use insecticides because of the danger of toxins getting in your food. You know that chemical engineers work to create effective insect repellents that are safe. Your challenge is to act as a chemical engineer and create an effective but safe ant repellent made of natural substances.*
   - Groups should complete a Need to Know Chart (in the Ask section of Lesson 3.1 My Engineering Journal) indicating what they know from reading the scenario, what they need to know to help solve the problem, and what they need to do. Students should include the criteria and constraints of the challenge in the "know" portion of the chart.
   - As a class, discuss environmental issues caused by pesticides. Students should research natural pesticides to help inform them of the best substance to create. Alternatively, before designing an insecticide, students could test individual substances from the material list to see which ones were best at inhibiting ants. They would do this using a controlled experiment as described below. This knowledge would help students prepare their solution.
   - Distribute Lesson 4.2 What Is a Controlled Experiment? and discuss with students how to design a science experiment. Explain that even though this is an engineering project, students will use a controlled experiment to test the created substance.
   - Review the parts of the controlled experiment with the class:
     - Independent Variable: The solution of natural substances.
     - Dependent Variable: Number of ants. More ants means the substance does not work as well.

    ◻ Control: In the ant experiment, there may be more than one control. A piece of paper with no substance added would be one control. Another would be the pesticide (optional) to use as a comparison to the safe insecticide solutions.

    ◻ Constants: These include the location, the material that attracts the ants (candy or fruit), and the amount of natural substance or pesticide on the cotton swab.

2. **Imagine:**
   - Have student groups revisit the Need to Know chart and add information as needed.
   - Student groups will brainstorm ideas for best pesticide contents and concentration. Students should agree upon the best solution or plan to complete the challenge.

3. **Plan:**
   - Have student groups develop a plan to create a natural insecticide that addresses the criteria. Each group should plan to create one solution of insecticide at four different concentrations. For example, one solution could be one part soap, two parts pepper sauce, and one part dish soap, while another solution could be two parts soap, one part pepper sauce, and one part dish soap.
   - Student groups should list the specific components (from a list of materials available for use) of their insecticide solution with exact measurements for each solution.

4. **Create:**
   - Student groups will follow their plans to create their agreed-upon solutions. You may want to give a time limit (15 minutes) and adjust as needed.
   - Students will use a controlled experiment to test solutions and compare the results across the different concentrations and with other groups.

5. **Improve:**
   - Have students reflect on the Improve questions from Lesson 3.1 My Engineering Journal.
   - Allow students time to improve their design and to retest. Students should take a picture or complete a drawing of their insecticide contents with the most effective concentration and add it to their engineering journal.

EXTENSION ACTIVITIES

- Have students create a graph of the total number of insects that were on the paper (dependent variable) versus each type of repellent (independent variable).

- Have students write a blog post explaining why natural substances should be used for pest control.

ASSESSMENT OBSERVATIONS

- Students should collaborate in a group to create a solution to the problem.
- Students should recognize the benefits of the engineering design process in solving problems.
- Students should design a controlled experiment, identifying the independent and dependent variables, as well as the control.

NAME: _____ DATE: _____

LESSON 4.2
Safe Insecticides

Problem/Challenge

You are planning a big picnic at the park. During a recent visit, you noticed that ants were everywhere, including on the picnic tables. You do not want to use insecticides because of the danger of toxins getting in your food. You know that chemical engineers work to create effective insect repellents that are safe. Your challenge is to act as a chemical engineer and create an effective but safe ant repellent made of natural substances.

Materials

- Area with ants
- White paper
- Paper cups to mix solutions
- Cotton swabs
- Small pieces of candy or fruit
- Materials for solutions: water, sugar, lemon juice, vinegar, baking soda, dish soap, hand soap, hot pepper sauce.

Criteria

- Your solutions must contain at least three substances.
- Prepare four different concentrations of the solution. For example, one solution could be one part soap, two parts pepper sauce, and one part dish soap, while another solution could be two parts soap, one part pepper sauce, and one part dish soap.

Constraints

- Use only the available materials given to your by your teacher.
- To limit liquid on white paper, transfer solution to paper using a cotton swab.

Procedure

1. In a paper cup, prepare a natural and safe substance that will repel ants.
2. Prepare three other strengths of that same solution in three more cups.
3. You will need to design a controlled experiment to test your substances. To do so, prepare five sheets of paper. One piece of paper will have no substance on it (the control), and the others will each have one solution.
4. Using a cotton swap, add one of the concentrations of repellent to the outside borders of a piece of paper.
5. Repeat step four for each of the other solutions.

76   *Thinking Like an Engineer* © Taylor & Francis.

Safe Insecticides, continued

6. Place your papers (control and four concentrations) in an area of active ants. Add a small piece of candy or fruit to the middle of each paper to encourage ants to come to the paper.
7. Count the number of ants on each paper after 5, 10, and 15 minutes. Record your results in the Ant Repellant Table below.
8. Note the effectiveness of each substance.

Ant Repellent Table

Solution	Number of Ants on Paper 5 minutes	Number of Ants on Paper 10 minutes	Number of Ants on Paper 15 minutes
No solution (control)			
Solution 1:			
Solution 2:			
Solution 3:			
Solution 4:			

Reflect

1. How did you act as an engineer in this challenge?

2. How did you act as a scientist in this challenge?

3. What else should be considered when eliminating or repelling insects?

LESSON 4.2

What Is a Controlled Experiment?

Directions: Read the definitions below. Then answer the questions that follow about your safe insecticide experiment.

> A **controlled experiment** is when the experimenter controls for other factors that may impact the experiment's results. Every part of the experiment is treated exactly the same except for the substance being tested. A controlled experiment includes the following:
> - **Independent Variable:** The variable that is changed by the experimenter.
> - **Dependent Variable:** The variable that is changed as a result of the independent variable.
> - **Control:** When the independent variable is not changed; the experimenter compares what happens in the control with what happens in the experiment.
> - **Constant:** What is kept the same in the experiment.

1. What is the independent variable?

2. What is the dependent variable?

3. What is the control?

4. What are the constants?

Thinking Like an Engineer © Taylor & Francis.

LESSON 4.3
BIOMEDICAL ENGINEER CHALLENGE

RESOURCES AND MATERIALS

- Lesson 3.1 My Engineering Journal
- Lesson 4.3 Prosthetic Hand
- Materials for prosthetic hand: straws, fishing line or thin string, rubber bands, paper clips, cardboard, tape, scissors, etc. (will vary based on design)
- Web resources:
  - Video: "How to Make a Mini Robotic Arm at Home out of Drinking Straws and Cardboard" by Yuri Ostr (https://www.youtube.com/watch?v=_N5A965XOOI)
  - Article: "Grasping With Straws: Make a Robot Hand Using Drinking Straws" by Science Buddies (https://www.sciencebuddies.org/science-fair-projects/project-ideas/Robotics_p001/robotics/drinking-straw-robot-hand#materials)

ESTIMATED TIME

3–4 hours

OBJECTIVES

In this lesson, students will:
- collaborate to solve a biomedical engineering problem, and
- design and create a working prosthetic limb.

CONTENT

In this lesson, students will act as biomedical engineers. Students will be working to design a prosthetic for someone in need. The lesson should follow the sequence of Ask, Imagine, Plan, Create, and Improve.

PRIOR KNOWLEDGE

Skills: collaboration, group work
Knowledge: robotics, prosthetics
Vocabulary: prosthetics, amputee, prototype, biomedical, anatomy, physiology, cells

INSTRUCTIONAL SEQUENCE

1. **Ask:**
   - Place students in groups of 3–4 and distribute Handout 4.3 Prosthetic Hand. Present the problem: *You are a biomedical engineer traveling to a third-world country to help children in need. Some children have lost their fingers, hands, and other limbs and are in need of prosthetics. You and your team will design and build a prototype of a working prosthetic for a child.*
   - Groups should complete a Need to Know Chart (in the Ask section of Lesson 3.1 My Engineering Journal) indicating what they know from reading the scenario, what they need to know to help solve the problem, and what they need to do. Students should include the criterion and constraint of the challenge in the "know" portion of the chart.
   - Discuss with the class the structure of body parts and their function in growth, survival, and behavior.
   - Tell students they will be researching different methods for building prosthetic limbs. Allow them to choose the best option for them and for the materials that you may have available (see Resources and Materials for examples).

2. **Imagine:**
   - Have student groups revisit the Need to Know chart and add information as needed.
   - Student groups should brainstorm ideas for the best way to design their prosthetic to meet the criterion. Students should agree upon the best solution or plan to complete the challenge.

3. **Plan:**
   - Have student groups develop a plan to design a prosthetic that addresses the criterion.
   - Student groups should construct a diagram of the prosthetic.

4. **Create:**
   - Student groups should follow their plans to create the prosthetic, using the resources available.
   - Give students a time limit (30–45 minutes) and adjust as needed.

5. **Improve:**
   - Have students reflect on the Improve questions from Lesson 3.1 My Engineering Journal.
   - Allow students time to improve their design to better meet the criterion.

EXTENSION ACTIVITIES

- Have students design a prosthetic on a digital fabrication site, such as Tinkercad (https://www.tinkercad.com). After designing the prosthetic, students could print a model using a 3-D printer.
- Students could participate in a service project such as Prosthetic Kids Hand Challenge (http://www.handchallenge.com) to design and print prosthetics for children.

ASSESSMENT OBSERVATIONS

- Students should work in a group to create a solution to the problem.
- Students should recognize the benefits of the engineering design process in solving problems.
- Students should evaluate the effectiveness of the prosthetic to perform routine tasks.
- Students should conclude that joints are necessary for movement in limbs.

LESSON 4.3
Prosthetic Hand

Problem/Challenge

You are a biomedical engineer traveling to a third-world country to help children in need. Some children have lost their fingers, hands, and other limbs and are in need of prosthetics. You and your team will design and build a prototype of a working prosthetic for a child.

Materials

The materials used will vary depending on your design. Options include straws, fishing line or thin string, rubber bands, paper clips, cardboard, tape, and scissors.

Criterion

Your robotic hand prototype must be able to pick up a can or other specified object.

Constraint

Your teacher may limit the type or number of materials you can use in your design.

UNIT 5

EXPLORE BEYOND YOUR WORLD LIKE AN ENGINEER

RATIONALE

In this unit, students will solve problems in relation to exploring beyond their world. Students will complete challenges in aerospace and computer engineering. Each design challenge provides a problem scenario, challenge, constraints, criteria, and materials representative of the theme. You may elect to do each challenge in the unit, select particular challenges for the class to complete, or allow groups of students to choose which challenge they would like to do. This is an opportunity for students to solve problems like engineers.

PLAN

In Lesson 5.1, students will act as aerospace engineers and be provided a real-world problem scenario to design and create a safe landing for a spacecraft. In Lesson 5.2, students will act as computer engineers in designing a virtual reality experience.

LESSON 5.1

AEROSPACE ENGINEER CHALLENGE

RESOURCES AND MATERIALS

- Lesson 3.1 My Engineering Journal
- Lesson 5.1 Smooth Landing
- Space landing materials (per group of 3–4; you may limit materials based on preferences):
  - 1 piece of cardstock or cardboard (approximately 4 x 5 in/10 x 13 cm)
  - 1 small paper or plastic cup (or item to house the astronaut)
  - Index cards (3 x 5 in/8 x 13 cm)
  - 2 astronaut figures (e.g., LEGOs, marbles, marshmallows)
  - Packing popcorn
  - Miniature marshmallows
  - Rubber bands
  - Plastic straws
  - Scissors
  - Tape

ESTIMATED TIME

3–4 hours

OBJECTIVES

In this lesson, students will:
- collaborate to solve an aerospace engineering problem,
- create a design and prototype of a spaceship, and
- test their prototypes for safety.

CONTENT

In this lesson, students will act as aerospace engineers. Students will be working to design a spacecraft to land two astronauts on the moon. The lesson should follow the sequence of Ask, Imagine, Plan, Create, and Improve.

PRIOR KNOWLEDGE

Skills: collaboration, group work
Knowledge: force, gravity, stability, structure
Vocabulary: rocket, space shuttle, force, gravity, acceleration, landing, aeronautics, solar system, shock absorbers

INSTRUCTIONAL SEQUENCE

1. **Ask:**
   - Place students in groups of 3–4 and distribute Lesson 5.1 Smooth Landing. Present the problem: *You are an aerospace engineer, and you are working with a team to design and create a better spacecraft that can safely land two astronauts on the moon.*
   - Groups should complete a Need to Know Chart (in the Ask section of Lesson 3.1 My Engineering Journal) indicating what they know from reading the scenario, what they need to know to help solve the problem, and what they need to do. Students should include the criteria and constraints of the challenge in the "know" portion of the chart.
   - Discuss gravity, force, and motion with the class. This would be a good time to discuss how shock absorbers can reduce the force of the strike on the ground when the spacecraft lands. You might also discuss how shock absorbers in cars work and ask students if they have ever been in a car during a bumpy ride. They should discuss how car rides affect passengers and what keeps them safe.

2. **Imagine:**
   - Have student groups revisit the Need to Know chart and add information as needed.
   - Student groups will brainstorm ideas for the best way to design their spacecraft to meet the criteria. Students should agree upon the best solution or plan to complete the challenge.

3. **Plan:**
   - Have student groups develop a plan to design the spacecraft that addresses the criteria.
   - Student groups should construct a diagram of the spacecraft.

4. **Create:**
   - Student groups will follow their plans to create and test the spacecraft (see Procedure in Lesson 5.1 Smooth Landing). You may limit materials used based on your preference. Students will need materials to make a spacecraft with a cabin and materials to act as a shock absorber.
   - You may want to give a time limit (30 minutes) and adjust as needed.

5. **Improve:**
   - Allow students time to improve their design to better meet the criteria.
   - Have students reflect on the Improve questions from Lesson 3.1 My Engineering Journal.

EXTENSION ACTIVITIES

- Have students test how high the spacecraft can fall while still keeping the astronauts safely inside.
- Have students test how many astronauts can remain safely in the cabin during landing.

ASSESSMENT OBSERVATIONS

- Students should work in a group to create a solution to the problem.
- Students should recognize the benefits of the engineering design process in solving problems.
- Students should recognize how shock absorbers help reduce the force of the landing.

LESSON 5.1
Smooth Landing[2]

Problem/Challenge

You are an aerospace engineer, and you are working with a team to design and create a better spacecraft that can safely land two astronauts on the moon.

Materials

- 1 piece of cardstock or cardboard (approximately 4 x 5 in/10 x 13 cm)
- 1 small paper or plastic cup (or item to house the astronaut)
- Index cards (3 x 5 in/8 x 13 cm)
- 2 astronauts (e.g., LEGOs, marbles, marshmallows)
- Packing popcorn
- Miniature marshmallows
- Rubber bands
- Plastic straws
- Scissors
- Tape

Criteria

- The two astronauts must remain safely in the spacecraft.
- The spacecraft must land upright.
- A cabin must be added to the spacecraft for astronauts.

Constraints

- You must only use the materials provided.
- The spacecraft cannot have a cover over the top.
- The astronauts need to be easily removed after landing.

Procedure

1. After designing and creating your spacecraft, you will test drop the spacecraft at various heights to determine if the shock absorbers reduce the impact of the landing and if the astronauts remain safely in the cabin. You should conduct three trials for each height.
2. Complete the following table indicating the following information for each trial and each height: astronauts remained in cabin (Y for Yes; N for No); spacecraft remained upright (Y for Yes; N for No).

---

2 Adapted from NASA and Design Squad, 2008. Copyright 2008 by NASA and Design Squad. Adapted with permission.

Smooth Landing, continued

	1 meter		2 meters		3 meters		4 meters	
	Astronauts Landed Safely (Y or N)	Spacecraft Remained Upright (Y or N)	Astronauts Landed Safely (Y or N)	Spacecraft Remained Upright (Y or N)	Astronauts Landed Safely (Y or N)	Spacecraft Remained Upright (Y or N)	Astronauts Landed Safely (Y or N)	Spacecraft Remained Upright (Y or N)
Trial 1								
Trial 2								
Trial 3								

LESSON 5.2

COMPUTER ENGINEER CHALLENGE

RESOURCES AND MATERIALS

- Lesson 3.1 My Engineering Journal
- Lesson 5.2 It's a Virtual World
- Student computers or tablets with CoSpaces Edu (https://cospaces.io/edu) or another 3-D software site
- Subscription to CoSpaces Edu (free)
- Virtual reality goggles and smartphone to be used with CoSpaces Edu app

ESTIMATED TIME

3–4 hours

OBJECTIVES

In this lesson, students will:
- collaborate to solve a computer engineering problem, and
- design and create a prototype for a virtual reality museum exhibit.

CONTENT

In this lesson, students will act as computer engineers. Students will be working to design a virtual reality museum exhibit. The lesson should follow the sequence of Ask, Imagine, Plan, Create, and Improve.

PRIOR KNOWLEDGE

Skills: collaboration, group work, ability to manipulate figures on the computer
Knowledge: virtual reality, museums
Vocabulary: museum, exhibits, virtual reality, artifacts, three-dimensional (3-D), hardware, software

INSTRUCTIONAL SEQUENCE

1. **Ask:**
   - Place students in groups of 3–4 and distribute Lesson 5.2 It's a Virtual World. Present the problem: *You are a computer engineer who has been hired by the Natural History Museum in Chicago to create a virtual reality museum exhibit. You must create a minimum of two rooms with three pictures or displays in each room.*
   - Explain that students can explore the content of their choice. They could connect the exhibit to any content they are studying. For example, students could create a virtual exhibit on different types of animals or plants, or they could create an exhibit representing different points in U.S. history.
   - Groups should complete a Need to Know Chart (in the Ask section of Lesson 3.1 My Engineering Journal) indicating what they know from reading the scenario, what they need to know to help solve the problem, and what they need to do. Students should include the criteria of the challenge in the "know" portion of the chart.
   - Students will use a computer application, such as CoSpaces Edu, to design the exhibit. For help creating a virtual reality exhibit, see https://blog.cospaces.io/create-your-own-vr-exhibition-b58c2f178e2. Tutorials can also be found at https://cospaces.io/edu/resources.html.

2. **Imagine:**
   - Have student groups revisit the Need to Know chart and add information as needed.
   - Student groups will brainstorm ideas for the best way to design their museum exhibits. Students should agree upon the best solution or plan to complete the challenge.

3. **Plan:**
   - Have student groups develop a plan to design two rooms of a museum exhibit that addresses the criteria.
   - Student groups should construct a diagram of the museum with the rooms of the exhibit.

4. **Create:**
   - Student groups will follow their plans to create the museum exhibit. You may want to give a time limit and adjust as needed.
   - Students should have opportunities to view other sites created by their classmates.

5. **Improve:**
   - Have students reflect on the Improve questions from Lesson 3.1 My Engineering Journal.
   - Allow students time to improve their design after viewing other groups' sites. Students should provide a link to their CoSpace in their engineering journal.

EXTENSION ACTIVITY

Have students narrate a museum tour or add other audio to the virtual reality experience.

ASSESSMENT OBSERVATIONS

- Students should work in a group to create a solution to the problem.
- Students should recognize the benefits of the engineering design process in solving problems.
- Students should be able to manipulate images in the computer application (CoSpaces) and design scaled models of exhibits.

LESSON 5.2

It's a Virtual World

Problem/Challenge

You are a computer engineer who has been hired by the Natural History Museum in Chicago to create a virtual reality museum exhibit. You must create a minimum of two rooms with three pictures or displays in each room.

Materials

- Computers or tablets with CoSpaces Edu (or another 3-D software site)
- Subscription to CoSpaces Edu
- Virtual reality goggles and smartphone to be used with CoSpaces Edu app

Criteria

- You must have at least two rooms.
- You must have three pictures/displays in each room.

UNIT 6

YOU CAN BE AN ENGINEER

RATIONALE

This unit provides students with varied opportunities to demonstrate their learning. Students will engage with real-world audiences as they present their work from this book and demonstrate how they embodied the role of engineers through solving problems using the engineering design process. Students will also collect additional information and data from engineers and engineering resources to create a living museum. Students will recognize the tremendous accomplishments of engineers and how society benefits from engineering products. Additionally, students will begin to view themselves as an engineer no matter their race, ethnicity, gender, or socioeconomic status.

PLAN

In this culminating unit, students will demonstrate their knowledge gained throughout the units. There are three lessons in this unit. In Lesson 6.1, students will present on one of their prototype designs from Units 3–5. In Lesson 6.2, students will research an engineering branch using a tic-tac-toe board. In Lesson 6.3, students will study and embody engineers to create a living museum.

LESSON 6.1

PRESENT TO A REAL-WORLD AUDIENCE

RESOURCES AND MATERIALS

- Lesson 6.1 Presentation Rubric
- Student computers or tablets with presentation software (will vary by student)

ESTIMATED TIME

120–150 minutes

OBJECTIVES

In this lesson, students will:
- create a presentation for a real-world audience about one of their prototype designs,
- explain how their prototype design met all of the requirements, and
- outline and communicate the path to developing the prototype.

CONTENT

Student groups will pick their favorite design and prototype from Units 3–5 and prepare a presentation for a formal audience. Students may choose their presentation format (e.g., video presentation, oral presentation, brochure, e-book, etc.). This lesson is flexible and can be used with any of the challenges in Units 3–5.

Ideally, the formal audience would consist of practicing engineers, business owners, and/or personnel from colleges of engineering. If securing a real-world audience is difficult, consider using Skype to virtually connect with an audience. Alternatively, students can present to other teachers, classrooms, administrators, or families.

PRIOR KNOWLEDGE

Knowledge: engineering design process
Skills: group work, using presentation software
Vocabulary: presentation, formal audience

INSTRUCTIONAL SEQUENCE

1. Introduce the project: Student groups will prepare a presentation about their engineering challenge and the process they used to create a prototype. This should include each step of the engineering design process: Ask, Imagine, Plan, Create, and Improve. Students should address their difficulties in completing the design and their successes.
2. Give student groups a choice in their mode of presentation, including digital and/or poster presentations. Students should also have a choice in their presentation format. They could present their information as an advertisement or an infomercial. They could also prepare the presentation as a training session for budding engineers.
3. Have all student groups present. Distribute Lesson 6.1 Presentation Rubric and have students self-critique their presentations.

EXTENSION ACTIVITY

Adapt the engineering challenges and projects for a local science fair. The students could prepare two different prototypes and test which one best meets the requirements as stated in each challenge.

ASSESSMENT OBSERVATIONS

- Student presentation is clear and professional.
- Students can explain the engineering design process.
- Students can explain their design and how it meets the requirements of the challenge.

LESSON 6.1

Presentation Rubric

	Senior Engineer	Engineer	Intermediate Engineer	Engineer in Training	Self-Assessment (Indicate what level of engineer you think you are and why you should be scored at that level.)
Organization	Presentation is organized with a discussion of the problem and challenge. Presentation guides audience through the engineering design process (Ask, Imagine, Plan, Create, and Improve). There is a clear path to solving the problem and creating and improving the design and prototype.	Presentation is organized with a discussion of the problem and challenge. Presentation guides audience through the engineering design process (Ask, Imagine, Plan, Create, and Improve). There is a somewhat clear path to solving the problem and creating and improving the design and prototype.	Presentation is organized with a discussion of the problem and challenge. Presentation guides audience through the engineering design process (Ask, Imagine, Plan, Create, and Improve). There is a vague path to solving the problem and creating and improving the design and prototype.	More than one requirement is missing. The presentation does not guide the audience through the engineering design process (Ask, Imagine, Plan, Create, and Improve). The path to solving the problem and creating and improving the design and prototype is unclear.	
Creativity	The presentation is detailed and creative in format, using available materials to engage the audience.	The presentation is detailed and creative in format and is somewhat engaging to the audience.	The presentation is detailed but lacks creativity and is not engaging to the audience.	The presentation lacks detail and creativity and fails to engage the audience.	
Knowledge and Skills	Presentation demonstrates accurate and extensive knowledge of the specific engineering field and the engineering design process.	Presentation demonstrates accurate knowledge of the specific engineering field and the engineering design process.	Presentation demonstrates mostly accurate knowledge of the specific engineering field and the engineering design process.	Presentation does not demonstrate accurate knowledge of the specific engineering field and the engineering design process.	

Thinking Like an Engineer © Taylor & Francis.

Presentation Rubric, continued

	Senior Engineer	Engineer	Intermediate Engineer	Engineer in Training	Self-Assessment (Indicate what level of engineer you think you are and why you should be scored at that level.)
Dispositions and Connections	Presentation includes the challenges and successes of completing the design. Presentation also makes detailed connections about how the engineering design process can be used to solve problems in the real world.	Presentation includes the challenges and successes of completing the design. Presentation also makes some connections about how the engineering design process can be used to solve problems in the real world.	Presentation includes either the challenges or successes of completing the design. Presentation also makes some connections about how the engineering design process can be used to solve problems in the real world.	Presentation either lacks the challenges/successes or does not make a connection about how the engineering design process can be used to solve problems in the real world.	
Comments and Concerns	Write one sentence stating what you learned from this project.

Write a question you have about this project. | | | | |
| **Teacher Comments** | | | | | |

LESSON 6.2

ENGINEERING BRANCH PROJECT

RESOURCES AND MATERIALS

- Lesson 6.2 Engineering Branch Project
- Students computers or tablets with Internet access

ESTIMATED TIME

3–5 days

OBJECTIVES

In this lesson, students will:
- collect and analyze data and information about engineering,
- determine contributions of engineers to society,
- relate challenges that engineers may face in solving problems, and
- evaluate the effectiveness of the engineering design process in solving problems.

CONTENT

Students will choose one square from each column in the tic-tac-toe board. One column has two choices for students to collect "real" data from practicing engineers. This would be optimal and could be done earlier in the curriculum (see Unit 2, Lesson 2.2) when students are meeting with practicing engineers. Through this choice board, students should obtain new information from research and data collection to formulate opinions on engineering as a career field.

PRIOR KNOWLEDGE

Knowledge/skills: speaking, listening, information about engineers and engineering, data collection and summary of findings, engineering design process, computer, research

Vocabulary: contributions, engineering

INSTRUCTIONAL SEQUENCE

1. Introduce the project and distribute Lesson 6.2 Engineering Branch Project. Explain to students that they will be collecting some more information about engineers to help with an upcoming project (Lesson 6.3). This will include data to be collected from engineers and/or engineering websites, as well as information about engineering accomplishments and where they occurred. Much of this information can be found in the resources in Lesson 2.1 Engineering Career Resources. Guide students to appropriate websites and assist them in making contact with practicing engineers from the community or online. Practice safety precautions when allowing students to use outside resources.

2. Individual students will choose one square from each column in the tic-tac-toe board to complete. (*Note.* Although intended to be an individual project, this project may also be completed in groups if desired.)

3. After students complete the project, they should organize their findings in a presentation format. This would be an ideal opportunity for students to compile their information from this project into a digital book through Book Creator or another source. The book could be shared with other audiences (e.g., classes, practicing engineers, families, etc.).

EXTENSION ACTIVITY

Have students respond to the following prompt, indicating why their chosen field of engineering is important to society: *A local newspaper station reports that your favorite field of engineering is no longer needed in society. Write a letter to the editor of the local newspaper defending your field and explaining its importance to society. Include accomplishments from the field and future endeavors.*

ASSESSMENT OBSERVATION

Students should accurately identify engineering contributions to society, timelines, and geographical areas of contribution.

LESSON 6.2

Engineering Branch Project

Directions: Answer the following questions, and then follow the directions for completing the tic-tac-toe board.

1. What branch of engineering are you interested in studying?

2. What are three tasks of engineers who work in this branch of engineering?

    a. _____

    b. _____

    c. _____

3. Where do these engineers typically work?

4. What educational path would you need to take to become this kind of engineer?

Thinking Like an Engineer © Taylor & Francis.

Engineering Branch Project, continued

Final Presentation

Choose one square from each column of the tic-tac-toe board. In the final presentation, using one of the choices of media, you will provide information about your engineering field and its contributions to society. A strong presentation will include both real data collection and Internet research.

Data Collection	Contributions to Society	Be an Engineer
Interview an engineer in your chosen branch of engineering. Develop questions to ask the engineer and record your interview. Provide a summary of your findings.	Identify and describe contributions of a famous person in your branch of engineering.	Write a journal entry from the point of view of a famous engineer as he or she encounters obstacles in his or her design.
Create a Google Survey and submit it to engineers in your chosen branch. Collect and represent the data in a table or graph.	Create a timeline of contributions from your branch of engineering (could be an interactive digital timeline).	Write a letter to your ELA teacher convincing him or her that you should use the engineering design process in your writing preparation.
Use approved Internet resources to collect information about your chosen field of engineering and its contributions to society.	Create a digital map (U.S. or world) highlighting areas with significant engineering accomplishments in your selected field (e.g., the Golden Gate Bridge).	Select five objects in your classroom and research how they were invented.

LESSON 6.3

BE AN ENGINEER!

RESOURCES AND MATERIALS

- Lesson 6.3: Living Museum
- Materials for a living museum (will vary depending on the student)
- Student computers or tablets with Internet access
- Web resources:
  - "Hall of Fame" by Edison Tech Center (http://www.edisontechcenter. org/HallofFame.html)
  - "5 Famous Women in Engineering" by Dorothy Crouch (https://stem jobs.com/famous-women-in-engineering)
  - "The 10 Greatest Engineers of All Time" by Dean McClements (https:// newengineer.com/insight/the-10-greatest-engineers-of-all-time-1100231)

ESTIMATED TIME

1–2 days

OBJECTIVE

In this lesson, students will prepare and present a living museum in which they portray engineers and describe their contributions to society.

CONTENT

Students will research engineers and some of their famous contributions to society. Additionally, students will participate in a living museum as engineers and will describe their contributions to society. Ideally, students could present the living museum at a parent night.

PRIOR KNOWLEDGE

Knowledge/skills: speaking, listening, information about their engineer
Vocabulary: museum, artifacts

INSTRUCTIONAL SEQUENCE

1. Tell students they will be preparing a living museum of engineers. Preparation will involve researching the characteristics and accomplishments of an engineer of their choice. Distribute Lesson 6.3 Living Museum to guide students in their research. Information from their tic-tac-toe board (see Lesson 6.2) may be helpful.
2. Students will dress up and portray their selected engineers. This portrayal could involve something as simple as a poster board decorated with information about the engineer with an area cut out for a student's face. Alternately, students could dress up in clothing matching the time period in which their engineers lived. Encourage them to be creative.
3. Students should prepare a 2-minute speech about their engineer with the following information:
   - Demographic information, including where the engineer is from, where he or she went to school, and any interesting facts about the engineer.
   - Why did the engineer enter the field of engineering?
   - What is the engineer's greatest accomplishment in the field of engineering?

4. Students who are not comfortable with oral presentations could choose to create a digital presentation to be displayed at the living museum or a type of display that contains photographs and copies of pertinent information, such as patents.

EXTENSION ACTIVITY

Students could conduct a science, technology, engineering, and mathematics (STEM) night where they are able to lead other students and parents through engineering challenges. They would portray their engineer as they lead their audience through a problem-solving activity.

ASSESSMENT OBSERVATIONS

- Students should choose engineers from diverse and underrepresented populations, incorporating racial and gender diversity.
- Students' costumes and/or displays should reflect the pertinent information they have learned about their engineers.

LESSON 6.3
Living Museum

Directions: Using the resources below, choose a famous engineer from your chosen field. Then research your engineer. You may use a separate sheet of paper to record your answers. You will use the information you gather to create an oral presentation for your living museum.

Resources

- "Hall of Fame" by Edison Tech Center (http://www.edisontechcenter.org/HallofFame.html)
- "5 Famous Women in Engineering" by Dorothy Crouch (https://stemjobs.com/famous-women-in-engineering)
- "The 10 Greatest Engineers of All Time" (https://newengineer.com/insight/the-10-greatest-engineers-of-all-time-1100231)

Questions

1. Where was the engineer born and raised?
2. What is the date of birth and date of death (if deceased) of your engineer?
3. What is the gender and race of the engineer?
4. Describe the engineer's family.
5. Did the engineer go to college to get an engineering degree? If so, where? If not, how did he or she become an engineer?
6. Why did the engineer enter the field of engineering?
7. What was the engineer's greatest professional accomplishment?
8. Why is the engineer famous?
9. What is the engineer's greatest professional failure?

Presentation

You will prepare a 2-minute presentation to portray your engineer at the living museum. You can dress up as your engineer or make a poster about the engineer with a cutout for your face. Your presentation should inform audiences of the answers to the questions above. The following is an example presentation for of a made-up engineer.

Hello, my name is Ginger Museum. I was born on September 22, 1943 in Denver, CO, but I grew up in St. Louis, MO. Thankfully, I am still living. I am a White female, and I have been married for 50 years. We have three children.

I attended the University of Oklahoma where I received my mechanical engineering degree. When I was young, I loved to build with LEGOs and decided that I wanted to design and create rides for amusement parks.

Living Museum, continued

My greatest accomplishment was the creation of the Triple Wave Roller Coaster at Twenty Flags Over America. The worst failure was when I prepared a prototype for a roller coaster at another amusement park and they chose someone else. But I did not give up; instead, I worked harder on my roller coaster prototype to make it even better.

REFERENCES

Dailey, D. (2017). Using engineering design challenges to engage elementary students across multiple content areas. *Gifted Child Today, 4*(3), 137–143.

Engineering is Elementary. (2018a). *The engineering design process.* Retrieved from https://www.eie.org/overview/engineering-design-process

Engineering is Elementary. (2018b). *Research instruments.* Retrieved from https://www.eie.org/engineering-elementary/research/research-instruments

Knight, M., & Cunningham, C. M. (2004). *Draw an Engineer Test (DAET): Development of a tool to investigate students' ideas about engineers and engineering.* Presented at the ASEE Annual Conference & Exposition, Salt Lake City, UT.

NASA & Design Squad. (2008). *A NASA/Design Squad challenge: Touchdown.* Retrieved from https://www.jpl.nasa.gov/edu/pdfs/touchdown_worksheet.pdf

National Research Council. (2012). *A framework for K–12 science education: Practices, crosscutting concepts, and core ideas.* Washington, DC: The National Academies Press.

NGSS Lead States. (2013). *Next generation science standards: For states, by states.* Washington, DC: The National Academies Press.

ABOUT THE AUTHOR

Debbie Dailey, Ed.D., is an assistant professor of teaching and learning at the University of Central Arkansas where she is the coordinator for the Gifted and Talented Program and director of STEMulate Engineering Academy, a summer camp for talented youth. Prior to moving to higher education, Debbie was a high school science teacher and gifted education teacher for 20 years. Debbie has authored and coauthored multiple journal articles, books, book chapters, and products focused on K–12 STEM and gifted education. She has delivered numerous professional development workshops and presentations at local, state, national, and international venues. Debbie currently serves as the secretary for the Council for Exceptional Children, The Association for the Gifted (CEC-TAG) and is the Chair-Elect for the NAGC STEM network. Debbie can be reached at ddailey@uca.edu.

NEXT GENERATION SCIENCE STANDARDS ALIGNMENT

Unit/Lesson	Next Generation Science Standards
Unit 1	3-5 ETS1-1. Define a simple design problem reflecting a need or a want that includes specified criteria for success and constraints on materials, time, or cost. 3-5 ETS1-2. Generate and compare multiple possible solutions to a problem based on how well each is likely to meet the criteria and constraints of the problem. 3-5 ETS1-3. Plan and carry out fair tests in which variables are controlled and failure points are considered to identify aspects of a model or prototype that can be improved. MS-PS2-2. Plan an investigation to provide evidence that the change in an object's motion depends on the sum of the forces on the object and the mass of the object.
Unit 3, Lesson 3.1	3-5 ETS1-1. Define a simple design problem reflecting a need or a want that includes specified criteria for success and constraints on materials, time, or cost. 3-5 ETS1-2. Generate and compare multiple possible solutions to a problem based on how well each is likely to meet the criteria and constraints of the problem. 3-5 ETS1-3. Plan and carry out fair tests in which variables are controlled and failure points are considered to identify aspects of a model or prototype that can be improved. MS-PS2-2. Plan an investigation to provide evidence that the change in an object's motion depends on the sum of the forces on the object and the mass of the object.

Unit/Lesson	Next Generation Science Standards
Unit 3, Lesson 3.2	3-5 ETS1-1. Define a simple design problem reflecting a need or a want that includes specified criteria for success and constraints on materials, time, or cost. 3-5 ETS1-2. Generate and compare multiple possible solutions to a problem based on how well each is likely to meet the criteria and constraints of the problem. 3-5 ETS1-3. Plan and carry out fair tests in which variables are controlled and failure points are considered to identify aspects of a model or prototype that can be improved. 4-PS3.4. Apply scientific ideas to design, test, and refine a device that converts energy from one form to another.
Unit 3, Lesson 3.3	3-5 ETS1-1. Define a simple design problem reflecting a need or a want that includes specified criteria for success and constraints on materials, time, or cost. 3-5 ETS1-2. Generate and compare multiple possible solutions to a problem based on how well each is likely to meet the criteria and constraints of the problem. 3-5 ETS1-3. Plan and carry out fair tests in which variables are controlled and failure points are considered to identify aspects of a model or prototype that can be improved. 4 PS3-1. Use evidence to construct an explanation relating the speed of an object to the energy of that object. 5 PS2-1. Support an argument that the gravitational force exerted by Earth on objects is directed down. MS-PS2-2. Plan an investigation to provide evidence that the change in an object's motion depends on the sum of the forces on the object and the mass of the object.
Unit 4, Lesson 4.1	3-5 ETS1-1. Define a simple design problem reflecting a need or a want that includes specified criteria for success and constraints on materials, time, or cost. 3-5 ETS1-2. Generate and compare multiple possible solutions to a problem based on how well each is likely to meet the criteria and constraints of the problem. 3-5 ETS1-3. Plan and carry out fair tests in which variables are controlled and failure points are considered to identify aspects of a model or prototype that can be improved. 5-ESS3-1. Obtain and combine information about ways individual communities use science ideas to protect the Earth's resources and environment. 5-ESS2.2. Describe and graph the amounts and percentages of water and fresh water in various reservoirs to provide evidence about the distribution of water on Earth.

Unit/Lesson	Next Generation Science Standards
Unit 4, Lesson 4.2	3-5 ETS1-1. Define a simple design problem reflecting a need or a want that includes specified criteria for success and constraints on materials, time, or cost. 3-5 ETS1-2. Generate and compare multiple possible solutions to a problem based on how well each is likely to meet the criteria and constraints of the problem. 3-5 ETS1-3. Plan and carry out fair tests in which variables are controlled and failure points are considered to identify aspects of a model or prototype that can be improved. 5-PS1-4. Measure and graph quantities to provide evidence that regardless of the type of change that occurs when heating, cooling, or mixing substances, the total weight of matter is conserved. 5-PS1-3. Make observations and measurements to identify materials based on their properties.
Unit 4, Lesson 4.3	3-5 ETS1-1 Define a simple design problem reflecting a need or a want that includes specified criteria for success and constraints on materials, time, or cost. 3-5 ETS1-2 Generate and compare multiple possible solutions to a problem based on how well each is likely to meet the criteria and constraints of the problem. 3-5 ETS1-3 Plan and carry out fair tests in which variables are controlled and failure points are considered to identify aspects of a model or prototype that can be improved. 4-LS1-1 Construct an argument that plants and animals have internal and external structures that function to support survival, growth, behavior, and reproduction. MS-LS1-4 Use argument supported by evidence for how the body is a system of interacting subsystems composed of groups of cells.
Unit 5, Lesson 5.1	3-5 ETS1-1 Define a simple design problem reflecting a need or a want that includes specified criteria for success and constraints on materials, time, or cost. 3-5 ETS1-2 Generate and compare multiple possible solutions to a problem based on how well each is likely to meet the criteria and constraints of the problem. 3-5 ETS1-3 Plan and carry out fair tests in which variables are controlled and failure points are considered to identify aspects of a model or prototype that can be improved. MS-PS2-2 Plan an investigation to provide evidence that the change in an object's motion depends on the sum of the forces on the object and the mass of the object.
Unit 5, Lesson 5.2	3-5 ETS1-1. Define a simple design problem reflecting a need or a want that includes specified criteria for success and constraints on materials, time, or cost. 3-5 ETS1-2. Generate and compare multiple possible solutions to a problem based on how well each is likely to meet the criteria and constraints of the problem. 3-5 ETS1-3. Plan and carry out fair tests in which variables are controlled and failure points are considered to identify aspects of a model or prototype that can be improved.

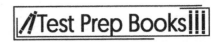

Table of Contents

//Test Prep Books!!!

Quick Overview

As you draw closer to taking your exam, effective preparation becomes more and more important. Thankfully, you have this study guide to help you get ready. Use this guide to help keep your studying on track and refer to it often.

This study guide contains several key sections that will help you be successful on your exam. The guide contains tips for what you should do the night before and the day of the test. Also included are test-taking tips. Knowing the right information is not always enough. Many well-prepared test takers struggle with exams. These tips will help equip you to accurately read, assess, and answer test questions.

A large part of the guide is devoted to showing you what content to expect on the exam and to helping you better understand that content. In this guide are practice test questions so that you can see how well you have grasped the content. Then, answer explanations are provided so that you can understand why you missed certain questions.

Don't try to cram the night before you take your exam. This is not a wise strategy for a few reasons. First, your retention of the information will be low. Your time would be better used by reviewing information you already know rather than trying to learn a lot of new information. Second, you will likely become stressed as you try to gain a large amount of knowledge in a short amount of time. Third, you will be depriving yourself of sleep. So be sure to go to bed at a reasonable time the night before. Being well-rested helps you focus and remain calm.

Be sure to eat a substantial breakfast the morning of the exam. If you are taking the exam in the afternoon, be sure to have a good lunch as well. Being hungry is distracting and can make it difficult to focus. You have hopefully spent lots of time preparing for the exam. Don't let an empty stomach get in the way of success!

When travelling to the testing center, leave earlier than needed. That way, you have a buffer in case you experience any delays. This will help you remain calm and will keep you from missing your appointment time at the testing center.

Be sure to pace yourself during the exam. Don't try to rush through the exam. There is no need to risk performing poorly on the exam just so you can leave the testing center early. Allow yourself to use all of the allotted time if needed.

Remain positive while taking the exam even if you feel like you are performing poorly. Thinking about the content you should have mastered will not help you perform better on the exam.

Once the exam is complete, take some time to relax. Even if you feel that you need to take the exam again, you will be well served by some down time before you begin studying again. It's often easier to convince yourself to study if you know that it will come with a reward!

Test-Taking Strategies

1. Predicting the Answer

When you feel confident in your preparation for a multiple-choice test, try predicting the answer before reading the answer choices. This is especially useful on questions that test objective factual knowledge. By predicting the answer before reading the available choices, you eliminate the possibility that you will be distracted or led astray by an incorrect answer choice. You will feel more confident in your selection if you read the question, predict the answer, and then find your prediction among the answer choices. After using this strategy, be sure to still read all of the answer choices carefully and completely. If you feel unprepared, you should not attempt to predict the answers. This would be a waste of time and an opportunity for your mind to wander in the wrong direction.

2. Reading the Whole Question

Too often, test takers scan a multiple-choice question, recognize a few familiar words, and immediately jump to the answer choices. Test authors are aware of this common impatience, and they will sometimes prey upon it. For instance, a test author might subtly turn the question into a negative, or he or she might redirect the focus of the question right at the end. The only way to avoid falling into these traps is to read the entirety of the question carefully before reading the answer choices.

3. Looking for Wrong Answers

Long and complicated multiple-choice questions can be intimidating. One way to simplify a difficult multiple-choice question is to eliminate all of the answer choices that are clearly wrong. In most sets of answers, there will be at least one selection that can be dismissed right away. If the test is administered on paper, the test taker could draw a line through it to indicate that it may be ignored; otherwise, the test taker will have to perform this operation mentally or on scratch paper. In either case, once the obviously incorrect answers have been eliminated, the remaining choices may be considered. Sometimes identifying the clearly wrong answers will give the test taker some information about the correct answer. For instance, if one of the remaining answer choices is a direct opposite of one of the eliminated answer choices, it may well be the correct answer. The opposite of obviously wrong is obviously right! Of course, this is not always the case. Some answers are obviously incorrect simply because they are irrelevant to the question being asked. Still, identifying and eliminating some incorrect answer choices is a good way to simplify a multiple-choice question.

4. Don't Overanalyze

Anxious test takers often overanalyze questions. When you are nervous, your brain will often run wild, causing you to make associations and discover clues that don't actually exist. If you feel that this may be a problem for you, do whatever you can to slow down during the test. Try taking a deep breath or counting to ten. As you read and consider the question, restrict yourself to the particular words used by the author. Avoid thought tangents about what the author *really* meant, or what he or she was *trying* to say. The only things that matter on a multiple-choice test are the words that are actually in the question. You must avoid reading too much into a multiple-choice question, or supposing that the writer meant something other than what he or she wrote.

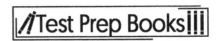

5. No Need for Panic

It is wise to learn as many strategies as possible before taking a multiple-choice test, but it is likely that you will come across a few questions for which you simply don't know the answer. In this situation, avoid panicking. Because most multiple-choice tests include dozens of questions, the relative value of a single wrong answer is small. As much as possible, you should compartmentalize each question on a multiple-choice test. In other words, you should not allow your feelings about one question to affect your success on the others. When you find a question that you either don't understand or don't know how to answer, just take a deep breath and do your best. Read the entire question slowly and carefully. Try rephrasing the question a couple of different ways. Then, read all of the answer choices carefully. After eliminating obviously wrong answers, make a selection and move on to the next question.

6. Confusing Answer Choices

When working on a difficult multiple-choice question, there may be a tendency to focus on the answer choices that are the easiest to understand. Many people, whether consciously or not, gravitate to the answer choices that require the least concentration, knowledge, and memory. This is a mistake. When you come across an answer choice that is confusing, you should give it extra attention. A question might be confusing because you do not know the subject matter to which it refers. If this is the case, don't eliminate the answer before you have affirmatively settled on another. When you come across an answer choice of this type, set it aside as you look at the remaining choices. If you can confidently assert that one of the other choices is correct, you can leave the confusing answer aside. Otherwise, you will need to take a moment to try to better understand the confusing answer choice. Rephrasing is one way to tease out the sense of a confusing answer choice.

7. Your First Instinct

Many people struggle with multiple-choice tests because they overthink the questions. If you have studied sufficiently for the test, you should be prepared to trust your first instinct once you have carefully and completely read the question and all of the answer choices. There is a great deal of research suggesting that the mind can come to the correct conclusion very quickly once it has obtained all of the relevant information. At times, it may seem to you as if your intuition is working faster even than your reasoning mind. This may in fact be true. The knowledge you obtain while studying may be retrieved from your subconscious before you have a chance to work out the associations that support it. Verify your instinct by working out the reasons that it should be trusted.

8. Key Words

Many test takers struggle with multiple-choice questions because they have poor reading comprehension skills. Quickly reading and understanding a multiple-choice question requires a mixture of skill and experience. To help with this, try jotting down a few key words and phrases on a piece of scrap paper. Doing this concentrates the process of reading and forces the mind to weigh the relative importance of the question's parts. In selecting words and phrases to write down, the test taker thinks about the question more deeply and carefully. This is especially true for multiple-choice questions that are preceded by a long prompt.

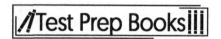

9. Subtle Negatives

One of the oldest tricks in the multiple-choice test writer's book is to subtly reverse the meaning of a question with a word like *not* or *except*. If you are not paying attention to each word in the question, you can easily be led astray by this trick. For instance, a common question format is, "Which of the following is…?" Obviously, if the question instead is, "Which of the following is not…?," then the answer will be quite different. Even worse, the test makers are aware of the potential for this mistake and will include one answer choice that would be correct if the question were not negated or reversed. A test taker who misses the reversal will find what he or she believes to be a correct answer and will be so confident that he or she will fail to reread the question and discover the original error. The only way to avoid this is to practice a wide variety of multiple-choice questions and to pay close attention to each and every word.

10. Reading Every Answer Choice

It may seem obvious, but you should always read every one of the answer choices! Too many test takers fall into the habit of scanning the question and assuming that they understand the question because they recognize a few key words. From there, they pick the first answer choice that answers the question they believe they have read. Test takers who read all of the answer choices might discover that one of the latter answer choices is actually *more* correct. Moreover, reading all of the answer choices can remind you of facts related to the question that can help you arrive at the correct answer. Sometimes, a misstatement or incorrect detail in one of the latter answer choices will trigger your memory of the subject and will enable you to find the right answer. Failing to read all of the answer choices is like not reading all of the items on a restaurant menu: you might miss out on the perfect choice.

11. Spot the Hedges

One of the keys to success on multiple-choice tests is paying close attention to every word. This is never truer than with words like almost, most, some, and sometimes. These words are called "hedges" because they indicate that a statement is not totally true or not true in every place and time. An absolute statement will contain no hedges, but in many subjects, the answers are not always straightforward or absolute. There are always exceptions to the rules in these subjects. For this reason, you should favor those multiple-choice questions that contain hedging language. The presence of qualifying words indicates that the author is taking special care with his or her words, which is certainly important when composing the right answer. After all, there are many ways to be wrong, but there is only one way to be right! For this reason, it is wise to avoid answers that are absolute when taking a multiple-choice test. An absolute answer is one that says things are either all one way or all another. They often include words like *every*, *always*, *best*, and *never*. If you are taking a multiple-choice test in a subject that doesn't lend itself to absolute answers, be on your guard if you see any of these words.

12. Long Answers

In many subject areas, the answers are not simple. As already mentioned, the right answer often requires hedges. Another common feature of the answers to a complex or subjective question are qualifying clauses, which are groups of words that subtly modify the meaning of the sentence. If the question or answer choice describes a rule to which there are exceptions or the subject matter is complicated, ambiguous, or confusing, the correct answer will require many words in order to be expressed clearly and accurately. In essence, you should not be deterred by answer choices that seem excessively long. Oftentimes, the author of the text will not be able to write the correct answer without offering some qualifications and modifications. Your job is to read the answer choices thoroughly and completely and to select the one that most accurately and precisely answers the question.

13. Restating to Understand

Sometimes, a question on a multiple-choice test is difficult not because of what it asks but because of how it is written. If this is the case, restate the question or answer choice in different words. This process serves a couple of important purposes. First, it forces you to concentrate on the core of the question. In order to rephrase the question accurately, you have to understand it well. Rephrasing the question will concentrate your mind on the key words and ideas. Second, it will present the information to your mind in a fresh way. This process may trigger your memory and render some useful scrap of information picked up while studying.

14. True Statements

Sometimes an answer choice will be true in itself, but it does not answer the question. This is one of the main reasons why it is essential to read the question carefully and completely before proceeding to the answer choices. Too often, test takers skip ahead to the answer choices and look for true statements. Having found one of these, they are content to select it without reference to the question above. Obviously, this provides an easy way for test makers to play tricks. The savvy test taker will always read the entire question before turning to the answer choices. Then, having settled on a correct answer choice, he or she will refer to the original question and ensure that the selected answer is relevant. The mistake of choosing a correct-but-irrelevant answer choice is especially common on questions related to specific pieces of objective knowledge. A prepared test taker will have a wealth of factual knowledge at his or her disposal, and should not be careless in its application.

15. No Patterns

One of the more dangerous ideas that circulates about multiple-choice tests is that the correct answers tend to fall into patterns. These erroneous ideas range from a belief that B and C are the most common right answers, to the idea that an unprepared test-taker should answer "A-B-A-C-A-D-A-B-A." It cannot be emphasized enough that pattern-seeking of this type is exactly the WRONG way to approach a multiple-choice test. To begin with, it is highly unlikely that the test maker will plot the correct answers according to some predetermined pattern. The questions are scrambled and delivered in a random order. Furthermore, even if the test maker was following a pattern in the assignation of correct answers, there is no reason why the test taker would know which pattern he or she was using. Any attempt to discern a pattern in the answer choices is a waste of time and a distraction from the real work of taking the test. A test taker would be much better served by extra preparation before the test than by reliance on a pattern in the answers.

FREE DVD OFFER

Don't forget that doing well on your exam includes both understanding the test content and understanding how to use what you know to do well on the test. We offer a completely FREE Test Taking Tips DVD that covers world class test taking tips that you can use to be even more successful when you are taking your test.

All that we ask is that you email us your feedback about your study guide. To get your **FREE Test Taking Tips DVD**, email freedvd@studyguideteam.com with "FREE DVD" in the subject line and the following information in the body of the email:

- The title of your study guide.
- Your product rating on a scale of 1-5, with 5 being the highest rating.
- Your feedback about the study guide. What did you think of it?
- Your full name and shipping address to send your free DVD.

Introduction to the California Post Exam

Function of the Test

California POST (Peace Officer Standards and Training) administers the POST Entry-Level Law Enforcement Test Battery (PELLETB) to prospective officers for various law enforcement agencies in California. California law requires that law enforcement officers be able to read and write at a level sufficient to perform the job of a peace officer. This is determined by the use of the PELLETB or other professionally developed and validated test of reading and writing ability. Accordingly, the PELLETB tests language aptitude, with sections covering both writing ability and reading ability. PELLETB scores are used by California law enforcement agencies as an indicator of a candidate's readiness for a career in law enforcement. The PELLETB is typically administered before a prospective officer is admitted to a police academy, and can be used by agencies as part of their hiring decisions.

Test Administration

The test is usually given free to all California law enforcement applicants. Applicants may be directed to take the test by the law enforcement agency to which they are applying, or they may contact an agency directly and register to take the test through that agency. The test is offered frequently, but not at any set state-wide time or date. Instead, local agencies determine when and where to administer the test.

Test-takers can retake the test, but must wait at least one month after taking the test to take it again. Test-takers with disabilities may seek appropriate accommodations through the agency offering the PELLETB.

Test Format

The test must be completed within two hours and thirty minutes. The test is administered in a written format, and is comprised of 131 multiple-choice, fill-in-the-blank questions covering reading, writing, and reasoning.

Component	Sub-Test	Questions	Description
Reading	Comprehension	28	Answer questions about a passage
Reading	CLOZE	40	Fill in a passage's missing words from context
Reasoning	Reasoning	9	Analyze patterns to answer questions
Writing	Clarity	18	ID which sentence is clearest
Writing	Spelling	18	Fill blank with properly spelled word
Writing	Vocabulary	18	ID the best synonym

The reading section is broken down into two sub-tests, comprehension and the CLOZE. The reading comprehension section asks test-takers to read a brief passage and answer multiple choice questions about the meaning of the passage. The CLOZE, often considered the most difficult sub-test, involves a passage in which specific words have been removed. Test-takers must determine from context what word appropriately fills the blanks thereby created.

The writing section is comprised of three sub-tests, clarity, spelling, and vocabulary. In the clarity sub-test, test-takers must determine which of two sentences is written more clearly. In the spelling sub-test, they must pick the correctly spelled word from four choices. In the vocabulary sub-test, they must identify the best synonym for a given word from four choices.

Finally, the reasoning sub-test presents the test-taker with patterns of letters, numbers, or shapes. The test-taker must analyze the patterns and answer questions about them.

Scoring

Prospective law enforcement officers who complete the PELLETB will receive a score known as a "T-score." A T-score is a standardized score that fits the performance of test-takers to a normalized curve. The average test-taker will receive a T-score of 50, and each standard deviation above or below the average will get a score 10 points higher or lower than 50. There is no set passing score, as different agencies will use different criteria at different times. However, a typical agency might set a minimum score between 40 and 45 for admission to their academy. Scores are generally returned to the agency (not the applicant) within about two weeks, and the agencies are required to provide applicants with their results within 30 days.

Clarity

In today's law enforcement world, the ability to write clearly and effectively is an important skill. Written communications such as incident reports and arrest reports are an integral part of the job, and being able to produce clear, comprehensive communications is essential.

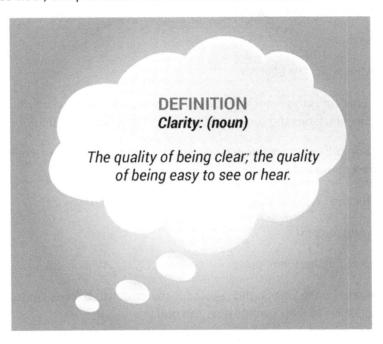

DEFINITION
Clarity: (noun)

The quality of being clear; the quality of being easy to see or hear.

Clear written communication is important in everyday life—particularly in law enforcement. Officers are often responsible for creating a variety of daily reports, and writing content that's clear and concise results in more effective communications.

This section of the study guide focuses on writing *clarity*. The definition of clarity is "the quality of being clear." In writing, this means that the content is focused and the writer's intention is clear in both word choice and sentence structure. Simply put, the writing is clear. Why is this important? Writers want their readers to understand exactly what they're saying and NOT misinterpret their words. In the same sense, readers want a clear understanding of what they're reading. The following section covers understanding writing clarity through basic grammar principles.

Subjects and Predicates

Subjects
Every complete sentence is made up of two parts: a subject and a predicate. The *subject* is *who* or *what* the sentence is about. There are three subject types: simple, complete, and compound.

A *simple subject* tells *who* or *what* the sentence is about without additional details. For example:

> The blue car won the race.

In this sentence, the simple subject is the word *car*.

A *complete subject* contains the simple subject and its modifiers. In writing, a *modifier* is a word or phrase that gives more detail about a part of the sentence. In this case, the modifier gives more information about the subject. When looking for a complete subject, first identify the verb or action word in the sentence (e.g., *run, jump, carried*), then ask to *who* or *what* the verb is referring. Look again at the previous example:

Sentence: The blue car won the race.

Identify the verb: *won*

Ask who or what won: *The blue car*

Answer: *The blue car* is the complete subject because it answers *what* won. Notice how the complete subject includes the simple subject (*car*) along with its modifier (*blue*).

If there's more than one subject in a sentence, it's called a *compound subject*. Look at the sentence below and identify the compound subject:

Sentence: John and I jumped over the huge puddle in the parking lot.

Identify the verb: *jumped*

Ask who or what jumped: *John and I*

Answer: *John and I* is the compound subject of the sentence because more than one subject can answer the question of *who* jumped over the puddle.

Predicates

In a sentence, the *predicate* usually tells something about the subject by describing what the subject does, is, or has. Similar to subjects, predicates are simple, complete, or compound.

A *simple predicate* is simply the verb. For example:

The dog ran into the busy road.

In this sentence, the simple predicate is the word *ran*.

A *complete predicate* contains the verb as well as its modifiers. In the example above, the complete predicate is *ran into the busy road*.

A *compound predicate* is when two or more words describe one subject. For example:

The flight was delayed and eventually canceled.

In this sentence, the compound predicate (*was delayed and eventually canceled*) provides two details about one subject (*The flight*).

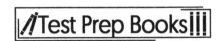

Modeling Subjects and Predicates in a Sentence Diagram

A *sentence diagram* makes it easier to identify the subject and predicate in a sentence. To create one, draw a long horizontal line with a short vertical line going through it. Write the subject of the sentence to the left of the vertical line and the predicate to the right. Here's an example:

The black pen | ran out of ink on the last page of the document.

    (*SUBJECT*)   (*PREDICATE*)

The vertical line divides the subject (*The black pen*) from the predicate (*ran out of ink*).

Subject-Verb Agreement

The basic rule of subject-verb agreement is that a *singular subject* (one person, place, or thing) requires a singular verb, while a *plural subject* (more than one person, place, or thing) needs a plural verb.

When a sentence is in the present tense and contains a singular subject, the singular verb usually ends with the letter *s*. For example:

Riley stacks the books on the shelf.

Since the subject (*Riley*) is singular, the verb needs to be singular (*stacks*). If the subject is plural, the verb must also be plural:

Riley and Nate stack the books on the shelf.

In this sentence the subject is plural (*Riley and Nate*) so the verb must be plural (*stack*). Subjects can be nouns (as above) or pronouns. When the subject is a singular pronoun such as *I* or *you*, the verb is also singular. In the case of *I* or *you*, though the verb is singular, it usually will not have an *s* on the end. For example:

Can *you call* for the pizza in ten minutes?

In this case the subject (*you*) is singular, so the verb (*call*) is also singular.

Subjects and verbs must also agree in point of view (POV) and verb tense (past, present, or future). The first-, second-, and third-person Point Of View pronouns (singular and plural) are shown below:

	First-Person POV	Second-Person POV	Third-Person POV
Singular Pronoun	*I*	*You*	*He/She/It*
Plural Pronoun	*We*	*You*	*They*

Using the chart above, look at the following examples of subject-verb agreement in relation to point of view and verb tense (in this case, present tense):

	Singular Verb	Plural Verb
First-Person POV	*I am swimming.*	*We are swimming.*
Second-Person POV	*You are swimming.*	*You are swimming.*
Third-Person POV	*He is swimming.*	*They are swimming.*

In each example above, the verb agrees with its singular or plural subject.

11

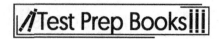

Words Between Subjects and Verbs

Interrupting words such as *of* and *to* are commonly used between subjects and verbs. For example:

> The lowest point *of* his career was yesterday, when he missed the penalty shot in the playoff game.

The subject here is *lowest point*, and the verb is *was*. Notice how the phrase *of his career* doesn't influence the verb *was*.

Compound Subjects

With a compound subject there's more than one subject (plural), so the verb must be plural. For example:

> *Mike and Vince* play basketball on Friday nights.

Notice how the compound subject (*Mike and Vince*) requires a plural verb (*play*) to agree.

Subjects Joined by *Or* or *Nor*

When singular subjects are joined by the words *or* or *nor*, they require a singular verb. If there are plural subjects, *the subject closest to the verb* determines if the verb is singular or plural. Here are examples of both:

> The table or the couch arrives tomorrow.

The singular verb (*arrives*) is used because the two singular subjects (*table* and *couch*) are joined by the word *or*.

> The table or the *couches* arrive tomorrow.

In this case, the plural verb (*arrive*) is used because the subject closest to the verb (*couches*) is plural.

Indefinite Pronouns *Either, Neither,* and *Each*

In a sentence, the words *either*, *neither*, and *each* act as singular subjects. For example:

> *Neither* of the printers *is* working properly.

Since the word *neither* acts as a singular subject, the verb (*is*) must also be singular.

The Adjectives *Every* and *Any* with Compounds

Compound words containing the adjectives *every* and *any* (e.g., everybody, anyone) act as singular subjects, so the verb must be singular. For example:

> *Everyone is* here for the surprise party!

Notice how the verb (*is*) is singular because the word *everyone* begins with *every*.

Collective Nouns

Collective nouns represent a group or collection of people, places, or things. Words such as *team*, *class*, *family*, and *jury* are all examples of collective nouns. When using a collective noun in a sentence, the verb is singular if the group is working together as a whole. For example:

> Their *family is* waiting for the dog to come home.

The collective noun *family* determines the singular verb *is* instead of *are.* A simple trick would be to replace the collective noun with a pronoun. In this case, replace *Their family* with *it*, since *family* refers to a single unit.

Plural Form and Singular Meaning

Some nouns are naturally plural. The words *acoustics*, *mathematics*, and *news* are all singular in meaning but plural in form. For plural nouns with singular meaning, the verb is singular. For example:

> The *news is* doing a special on male teachers in elementary education.

Notice how *news* seems plural but is actually singular. Therefore, it uses the singular verb *is.*

Complements

Nouns, pronouns, and adjectives can act as *complements*, providing details to complete the meaning of a sentence. These so-called "sentence completers" include predicate nominatives, predicate adjectives, direct objects, and indirect objects. It's important to note that both predicate nominatives and predicate adjectives follow *linking verbs* (e.g., *is, am, are, was, were, be, being, been*) that show no action.

Predicate Nominatives

Predicate nominatives are nouns or pronouns that rename or modify the subject and *follow a linking verb*. For example:

> My dog is a poodle.

In this sentence, the word *poodle* renames the subject (*dog*) and follows the linking verb (*is*).

Predicate Adjectives

Predicate adjectives are adjectives that rename or modify the subject and *follow a linking verb*. For example:

> My cat is lazy.

In this sentence, the word *lazy* is the predicate adjective because it modifies the subject (*cat*) and follows the linking verb (*is*).

Direct Objects

A *direct object* is a noun, pronoun, or phrase that follows an action verb and answers the question *what* or *who* about the verb. Though a sentence needs a subject and a verb to be complete, it doesn't always need a direct object. To find the direct object in a sentence, look at the following formula:

> Subject + Verb + *what*? or *who*? = Direct Object

Now, apply this formula to the following sentence:

Spike and Sheena chased the ball around the house.

Subject(s): *Spike and Sheena*

Verb: *chased*

Direct Object: *the ball*

Indirect Objects

An *indirect object* is a noun or pronoun that tells *to whom* or *for whom* the action of the verb is being done. A sentence must have a direct object to have an indirect object. When looking for the indirect object in a sentence, first find the verb and then ask the question *to whom* or *for whom*. For example:

Lucy passed the crayon to her friend.

In this sentence, the indirect object is *her friend* because it answers *to whom* Lucy *passed* (verb) *the crayon* (direct object).

Pronoun Usage

A *pronoun* is a word that takes the place of a noun. This section looks at the different ways that pronouns are used in sentences.

Pronoun-Antecedent Agreement

An *antecedent* is a word or phrase that typically comes first, followed by a pronoun that refers to it. The pronoun must agree with its antecedent in form (singular or plural). For example:

Singular Agreement:

The *package* was dropped off at my door, and *it* was very heavy.

Here the antecedent (*package*) is singular, so the pronoun (*it*) must also be singular.

Plural Agreement:

The *packages* were dropped off at my door, and *they* were very heavy.

In this example, the antecedent (*packages*) is plural, so the pronoun (*they*) must also be in plural form.

When there are *compound subjects* (more than one subject) in a sentence, test each pronoun individually with the verb to determine which one is correct. To do this, simply remove the first subject, read the sentence with the remaining pronoun, and decide which one sounds better. For example, look at these two sentences:

Mom and I are going to the park.

Mom and me are going to the park.

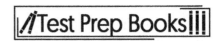

Delete the first subject (*Mom*) from the sentences and then read them both (*I am going to the park* and *me is going to the park*). Which one sounds better? Clearly the first sentence, so the pronoun *I* is the correct choice.

Pronoun Reference

A pronoun shouldn't confuse the reader about whom or what it's describing, and it should clearly refer to its antecedent. For example:

Unclear: The shovel and the pail floated away in the ocean, and it was long gone.

In this sentence, it can't be determined if the pronoun *it* refers to *the shovel* or *the pail*.

Clear: The pail floated away in the ocean, and it was long gone.

In this sentence, the pronoun *it* clearly refers to its antecedent, *the pail*.

Personal Pronouns

Personal pronouns can be in the subjective, objective, or possessive case:

Subjective Case: The pronoun replaces the subject of the sentence.

Objective Case: The pronoun functions as the object.

Possessive Case: The pronoun shows possession of something.

The table below provides examples of each personal pronoun case:

Subjective	Objective	Possessive
I	Me	Mine
You	You	Yours
He	Him	His
She	Her	Hers
It	It	Its
We	Us	Ours
They	Them	Theirs
*Who	*Whom	Whose

*The pronouns *who* and *whom* are often used incorrectly. Use the pronoun *who* when referring to the *subject* of the sentence. Use the pronoun *whom* when referring to the *object* of the sentence.

In the following sentence, identify each pronoun and its case:

The flowers grew in his garden.

The pronoun is *his,* and it's in the possessive case.

Can someone please tell them to turn the music down?

The pronoun is *them,* and it's in the objective case.

Melissa is a really good cook, and she uses only fresh ingredients.

The pronoun is *she,* and it's in the subjective case.

Sentence Structures

There are many ways to organize the words in a sentence to clarify ideas. The four main sentence structures are simple sentences, compound sentences, complex sentences, and compound-complex sentences. In writing, using a variety of these structures makes the style more effective.

Simple Sentences

A *simple sentence* is made up of one independent clause. An *independent clause* is a separate complete thought that can stand on its own, and contains a subject and a predicate. Simple sentences can have compound subjects or compound verbs, but they can only have one main thought. The following is an example of a simple sentence:

> The bus was late.

The singular subject is *bus*, and the predicate is *was late*, so the sentence is a complete thought.

Compound Sentences

A *compound sentence* uses a conjunction to join two independent clauses. *Conjunctions* are linking words such as *and, but, for, nor, or, so,* and *yet*. For example:

> Bradley waited for the bus, but the bus was late.

In this sentence there are two complete thoughts (*Bradley waited for the bus* and *the bus was late*) joined by the conjunction *but*. Therefore, this is a compound sentence.

Complex Sentences

A *complex sentence* consists of one independent clause and one or more dependent clauses. A *dependent clause* is a clause that contains a subject and a verb, but can't stand on its own as a sentence. Complex sentences often use words like *after, although, before, while, wherever, if,* and *since.* For example:

> Although she really enjoyed the opera, Mary was very tired by the end of the night.

The first word in the sentence (*Although*) immediately attracts the reader's attention. The dependent clause (*Although she really enjoyed the opera*) is followed by the independent clause (*Mary was very tired by the end of the night*), which makes this a complex sentence.

Compound-Complex Sentences

A *compound-complex sentence* has at least two independent clauses and at least one dependent clause. For example:

> Although she really enjoyed the opera, Mary was very tired by the end of the night, and she still had to walk home.

The dependent clause (*Although she really enjoyed the opera*) depends on both the first independent clause (*Mary was very tired by the end of the night*) and the second independent clause (*and she still had to walk home*).

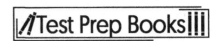

Sentence Fragments

A *sentence fragment* is an incomplete sentence that can't stand on its own. It's a dependent clause or phrase that looks like sentences but isn't. A sentence fragment may start with a capital letter and end with punctuation, but it isn't a complete thought. To revise a sentence fragment, either link the fragment to another sentence or add on to create a complete sentence. Look at the following example:

> I turned off the television. Because the phone was ringing.

> Fragment: *Because the phone was ringing.*

> Possible revisions:

>> I turned off the television because the phone was ringing.

>> Because the phone was ringing, I ran upstairs to answer it.

Dangling and Misplaced Modifiers

Dangling Modifiers

A *dangling modifier* is a word or phrase where the word it's supposed to modify is missing. In other words, it has nothing to modify. It can also be a dependent clause that's not logically related to the word it should modify. To correct a dangling modifier, connect it to the word it's to modify. For example:

> *Dangling*: Having designed the float for the parade, it will take six months to build it.

> *Revised*: Having designed the float for the parade, he expects to build it in six months.

In the revision, *Having designed* now correctly modifies the subject of the sentence (*he*).

Misplaced Modifiers

A *misplaced modifier* is word or phrase that's separated from the word that it's supposed to modify. Though a modifier can be put in more than one place within a sentence, the modifier should be clearly attached to the word it describes. For example:

> *Misplaced*: The dog almost chased the squirrel for an hour.

> *Revised*: The dog chased the squirrel for almost an hour.

In this example, the dog didn't *almost* chase the squirrel, it *did* chase the squirrel. The revised version of the sentence connects the word *almost* to the words *an hour,* which creates the clearest meaning of the sentence.

Run-On Sentences

A *run-on sentence* has two or more independent clauses that aren't connected by any punctuation. Instead, the sentence goes on and on without any pauses or stops. Here are some ways to correct a run-on sentence:

Add a comma and a coordinating conjunction:

>   *Incorrect*: I loaded the dishwasher can you drain the sink?

>   *Correct*: I loaded the dishwasher, so can you drain the sink?

Add a semicolon, colon, or dash (without a coordinating conjunction) when the two independent clauses are related to each other:

>   *Incorrect*: I went to the movies at the snack bar I bought candy.

>   *Correct*: I went to the movies; there I bought candy at the snack bar.

Separate the clauses by turning them into two separate sentences:

>   *Incorrect*: The grocery store was busy it quickly sold out of bread.

>   *Correct*: The grocery store was busy. It quickly sold out of bread.

Turn one of the independent clauses into a phrase:

>   *Incorrect*: The grocery store was busy it quickly sold out of bread.

>   *Correct*: The busy grocery store quickly sold out of bread.

Practice Questions

Directions: In each pair of sentences, select the sentence (a or b) that is written most clearly. Keep in mind the basic elements of grammar as they relate to writing clarity.

1.
   - a. Detective Shaw and Officer Boyd chases the suspect into the alley so he can't escape.
   - b. Detective Shaw and Officer Boyd chase the suspect into the alley so he can't escape.

2.
   - a. The jury is still out trying to reach a verdict.
   - b. The jury are still out trying to reach a verdict.

3.
   - a. The gun or the bullets was taken from the evidence locker without permission.
   - b. The gun or the bullets were taken from the evidence locker without permission.

4.
   - a. Officer Brady and me returned to the crime scene to interview the witnesses.
   - b. Officer Brady and I returned to the crime scene to interview the witnesses.

5.
   - a. Neither of the witness statements shows the time of the accident.
   - b. Neither of the witness statements show the time of the accident.

6.
   - a. The prisoner was able to escape. Because the cell door wasn't locked.
   - b. The prisoner was able to escape because the cell door wasn't locked.

7.
   - a. Having finished the police report, Officer Grant closed the case.
   - b. Having finished the police report, the case was closed.

8.
   - a. When the lawyer arrived late to court, the judge had good reason to reprimand her.
   - b. The judge had good reason to reprimand the lawyer when she arrived late to court.

9.
   - a. Who is taking the suspect downtown for questioning?
   - b. Who are taking the suspect downtown for questioning?

10.
   - a. The flashing police car's lights could be seen two blocks away.
   - b. The police car's flashing lights could be seen two blocks away.

11.

    a. Detective Reid finished collecting evidence at the crime scene. He placed each hair sample and carpet fiber in separate envelopes.

    b. Detective Reid finished collecting evidence at the crime scene he placed each hair sample and carpet fiber in separate envelopes.

12.

    a. In some states, guns injure more people than traffic accidents.

    b. In some states, more people are injured by guns than by traffic accidents.

13.

    a. Not everybody have the honesty, strength, and commitment it takes to become a law enforcement professional.

    b. Not everybody has the honesty, strength, and commitment it takes to become a law enforcement professional.

14.

    a. After graduating from high school, John's father suggested that he apply to the police academy.

    b. After John graduated from high school, his father suggested that he apply to the police academy.

15.

    a. Tonight's news has a story about an officer who apprehended an FBI fugitive during a routine traffic stop.

    b. Tonight's news have a story about an officer who apprehended an FBI fugitive during a routine traffic stop.

Answer Explanations

1. B: This sentence contains a compound subject, which means there's more than one subject (*Detective Shaw* and *Officer Boyd*). In subject-verb agreement, when the subject is plural the verb must also be plural (*chase*).

2. A: The subject (*jury*) is a collective noun and is treated as a singular subject. For proper subject-verb agreement, the singular subject must have a singular verb.

3. B: In proper subject-verb agreement, when two subjects are joined by the words *or* or *nor*, they usually take a singular verb. However, if one of those subjects is plural, *the subject closest to the verb* determines if the verb is singular or plural. Since the plural subject (*bullets*) is closest to the verb, the plural verb (*were*) is used.

4. B: This sentence contains a compound subject (more than one subject). The first subject is a noun (*Officer Brady*), while the second subject is a pronoun (*me* or *I*). To test which pronoun is correct, remove the first subject (*Officer Brady*), read the sentence with each pronoun, and then decide which sentence sounds better. In this case, the pronoun *I* is the best choice, so Choice *B* is correct.

5. A: The words *either*, *neither*, and *each* act as singular subjects in a sentence and therefore take a singular verb. *Neither* is the subject of this sentence, so it must take a singular verb (*shows*).

6. B: The first part of Choice *A* is a complete sentence, but the second part (*Because the cell door wasn't locked.*) is actually a sentence fragment. Though it looks like a sentence, because it begins with a capital letter and ends with punctuation, it is considered a fragment. A fragment is an incomplete sentence that can't stand on its own.

7. A: Choice *B* is an example of a dangling modifier, which is when the word that another word (or phrase) is supposed to modify is missing. In other words, the modifier has nothing to modify. In choice *B*, the *case* didn't finish the police report, a person did. In Choice *A*, by adding the name of the person who performed the action (*Officer Grant*), the dangling modifier is corrected.

8. A: In Choice *B*, it's unclear whether the pronoun *she* is referring to the judge or the lawyer arriving late to court. In Choice *A*, by rewriting the sentence, it becomes clear that *she* is the lawyer.

9. A: When using *that, which*, or *who* as the subject of a sentence, the verb is singular. Choice *A* uses the singular form of the verb (*is*).

10. B: This is an example of a misplaced modifier where a word or phrase is separated from the word that it's supposed to modify. In Choice *A*, the *police* is not what's *flashing,* the lights are. The modifier (*flashing*) should be attached to the word it's supposed to describe (*lights*). In Choice *B*, by moving the modifier, it now correctly modifies the word it should.

11. A: A run-on sentence has two or more independent clauses that aren't connected by punctuation, so the sentence goes on and on. Choice *B* is a run-on sentence because there is no punctuation to break up the independent clauses. By adding a period at the end of the first clause and capitalizing the beginning of the next, the run-on becomes two complete sentences.

12. B: Choice *A* lacks clarity, making it sound as if the *guns* are injuring both *people* and *traffic accidents*. Since *guns* can't injure *traffic accidents*, the sentence must be rewritten with greater clarity as done in Choice *B*.

13. B: Compound words that contain the adjectives *every* and *any* (e.g., <u>every</u>body, <u>any</u>one) are treated as singular subjects, so their verbs must also be singular. Since the word *everybody* is singular, its verb must be singular (*has*) as in Choice *B*.

14. B: In Choice *A* it's not clear who the subject of the introductory clause is, so it's unclear if *John* or *John's father* is the one who graduated from high school. Though the reader could guess what's actually meant, it's better for the sentence to be clear (as in Choice *B*) so there's no confusion about who graduated.

15. A: Some nouns like *news*, *measles*, and *mathematics* are all singular in meaning but plural in form. In this sentence, the word *news* seems plural but is actually singular. These *plural nouns with singular meaning* take a singular verb, so Choice *A* is correct with the use of the singular verb *has*.

Spelling

Police officers are expected to express themselves with authority. Choosing the best words for each situation is only part of this task. Being able to spell those words correctly is also crucial. For this reason, their aptitude for spelling is measured on the California POST. Consider, too, that accurate spelling helps to convey competence and professionalism.

The spelling test portion of the exam includes fifteen multiple-choice items, each featuring a sentence with one word omitted. The answer choices will present four different spellings of the same word, only one of which is correct. Test takers will be asked to identify the correct spelling.

Importance of Prefixes and Suffixes

The most common spelling mistakes are made when a *root word* (or a basic, core word) is modified by adding a prefix or a suffix to it. A *prefix* is a group of letters added to the beginning of a word, and a *suffix* is a group of letters added to the end of a word.

The prefixes usually change the meaning of the word. They might be negative or positive and signal time, location, or number. Note the spelling of the root word (or base word) does not change when adding a prefix.

Common Prefixes		
Prefix	**Meaning**	**Example**
dis-	not, opposite	disagree, disproportionate
en-, em-	to make, to cause	encode, embrace
in-, im-	in, into	induct
ir-, il-, im-	not, opposite	impossible, irresponsible
mis-	bad, wrongly	misfire, mistake
mono-	alone, one	monologue
non-	not, opposite	nonsense
over-	more than, too much	overlook
pre-	before	precede
post-	after	postmortem
re-	again, back	review
un-	not, opposite	unacceptable

A suffix can change the base word in two ways:

- Change numerical agreement: turns a singular word into a plural word (a singular witness becomes plural witnesses)

- Change grammatical function: turns one part of speech into another (noun to verb, verb to adverb), such as moderation, moderating, or moderately

Common Suffixes		
Suffix	**Meaning/Use**	**Example**
-able, -ible	able to	unbearable, plausible
-ance	state of being	significance
-al, -ial	relating to	lethal, testimonial, criminal
-ceed, -sede, -cede	go, go forward, withdraw, yield	exceed, recede, supersede
-ed	changes root word to past tense or past participle	called, played
-en	makes root word a verb	heighten, liven
-er	more, action, a person who does an action	clearer, sever, believer
-ful	full of	hateful, beautiful
-ian, -ite	person who does the action, part of a group	politician, meteorite
-ice, -ize	cause, treat, become	service, popularize
-ing	action	writing, playing
-ion, -tion	action or condition	celebration, organization
-ism	forms nouns referring to beliefs or behavior	Buddhism, recidivism
-ity, -ty	state of being	adversity, cruelty
-ive, -tive	state or quality	defensive, conservative
-less	without	tactless, nameless
-ly	in such a manner	poorly, happily
-ment	action	endorsement, disagreement
-ness	makes root word a noun referring to a state of being	weakness, kindness
-or	a person who does an action	moderator, perpetrator
-s, -es	makes root word plural	weights, boxes
-sion	state of being	admission, immersion
-y	made up of	moody, greasy

Doubling-Up Consonants (or Not)

When adding some suffixes (usually, *-ing*, *-sion*) to a root word that ends in one vowel followed immediately by one consonant, *double that last consonant.*

Base Word	Vowel/consonant	Suffix	Spelling Change
wrap	a, p	-ing	wrapping
canvas	a, s		canvassing
admit	i, t	-sion	admission

This rule does not apply to multi-vowel words, such as *sleep, treat,* and *appear.* When attaching a suffix that begins with a vowel to a word with a multi-letter vowel followed by a consonant, *do not double the consonant.*

Base Word	Multi-vowel, consonant	Suffix	Spelling
sleep	ee, p	-ing	sleeping
treat	ea, t	-ed	treated
appear	ea, r	-ance	appearance

Do *not* double the consonant if the root word already ends in a double consonant or the letter *x* (examples—*add/adding, fox/foxes*).

Words Ending with *y* or *c*

If a root word ends in a single vowel *y*, the *y* should be changed to i when adding any suffix, unless that suffix begins with the letter *i*. If a root word ends in a two-letter vowel, such as *oy, ay,* or *ey,* the *y* is kept.

Root Word	Ending	Suffix	Spelling Change
baby	y	-ed	babied
stymy	y		stymied
crony	y	-ism	cronyism
say	y	-ing	saying
annoy	oy	-ance	annoyance
survey	ey	-ing	surveying

In cases where the root word is a verb (ending with the letter *c*) and the suffix begins with an *e, i,* or *y,* the letter *k* is added to the end of the word between the last letter and the suffix.

Root Word	Ending	Suffix	Spelling Change
panic	ic	-ing	panicking
		-y	panicky
traffic	ic	-ed	trafficked
		-er	trafficker

Words with _ie_ or _ei_

There's an old saying "_I_ before _E_, except after _C_." There's also a second part to it:

> _I_ before _E_,
>
> Except after _C_,
>
> Or when sounded as _A_,
>
> As in _neighbor_ and _weigh_.

Here are a few examples:

- friend, wield, yield (i before e)
- receipt, deceive (except after c)
- _weight, freight_ (or when sounded as _a_)

Words Ending in _e_

Generally, the _e_ at the end of English words is silent or not pronounced (e.g., _bake_).

- If the suffix being added to a root word begins with a consonant, keep the _e_.
- If the suffix begins with a vowel, the final silent _e_ is dropped.

Root Word	Ending	Suffix	Spelling Change
waste remorse pause	silent _e_	-ful -s	wasteful remorseful pauses
reserve pause	silent _e_	-ation -ing	reservation pausing

Exceptions: When the root word ends in _ce_ or _ge_ and the suffix _–able_ or _–ous_ is being added, the silent final _e_ is kept (e.g., _courageous, noticeable_).

Words Ending with _-ise_ or _-ize_

Sometimes, it can be difficult to tell whether a word (usually a verb) should end in _–ise_ or _–ize_. In American English, only a few words end with _–ise_. A few examples are _advertise, advise,_ and _compromise._ Most words are more likely to end in _–ize._ A few examples are _accessorize, authorize, capitalize,_ and _legalize._

Words Ending with _-ceed, -sede,_ or _-cede_

It can also be difficult to tell whether a word should end in _–ceed, –sede,_ or _–cede._ In the English language, there are only three words that end with _–ceed: exceed, proceed,_ and _succeed._ There is only one word that ends with _–sede: supersede._

If a word other than _supersede_ ends in a suffix that sounds like _–sede,_ it should probably be _–cede._ For example: _concede, recede,_ and _precede._

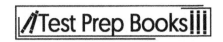

Words Ending in –able or –ible

In the English language, more words end in –able than in –ible:

- e.g., probable, actionable, approachable, traceable
- e.g., accessible, admissible, plausible

Words Ending in -ance or -ence

The suffixes -ance and -ence are added to verbs to change them into nouns or adjectives that refer to a state of being. For example, when -ance is added to the verb *perform*, *performance* is formed, referring to the act of performing.

Suffix	When to use	Example
-ance, -ancy, -ant	- When the root word ends in a *c* that sounds like *k* - When the root word ends in a hard *g*	- significance - arrogance - vacancy - extravagant
-ence, -ency, -ent	- When the root word ends in a *c* that sounds like *s* - When the root word ends in a *g* that sounds like *j*	- adolescence - convergence - contingency - convergent

Words Ending in -tion, -sion, or -cian

The suffixes –tion and –sion are used when forming nouns that refer to the result of a verb. For example, the result of to *abbreviate* something is an *abbreviation*. Likewise, if a person has *compressed* something, then there is a *compression*.

The suffix –cian is used when referring to a person who practices something specific. For example, the person who practices *politics* is a *politician*.

Words Containing -ai or -ia

Unfortunately, there isn't an easy-to-remember rhyme for deciding whether a word containing the vowels *a* and *i* should be spelled *ai* or *ia*. In this case, it's helpful to rely on pronunciation to determine the correct spelling.

The combination of *ai* is one sound, as in the words capt*ai*n and f*ai*nt.

The combination of *ia*, on the other hand, is two separate sounds, as in the words guard*ia*n and d*ia*bolical.

It's helpful to say the word out loud to decide which combination of the two vowels is correct.

Rules for Plural Nouns

Nouns Ending in -ch, -sh, -s, -x, or -z

When modifying a noun that ends in *ch, sh, s, x,* or *z* to its plural form, add *es* instead of the singular *s*. For example, *trench* becomes *trenches, ash* becomes *ashes, business* becomes *businesses, jukebox* becomes *jukeboxes,* and *fox* becomes *foxes.*

This rule also applies to family names. For example, the Finch family becomes the *Finches,* and the Martinez family becomes the *Martinezes.*

Nouns Ending in y or ay, ey, iy, oy, or uy

When forming plurals with nouns ending in the consonant *y,* the *y* is replaced with *-ies.* For example, *spy* becomes *spies,* and *city* becomes *cities.*

If a noun ends with a vowel before a *y,* the *y* is kept, and an *s* is added. For example, *key* becomes *keys,* and *foray* becomes *forays.*

Nouns Ending in f or fe

When forming plurals with nouns ending in *f* or *fe,* the *f* is replaced with *v,* and *es* is added. For example, *half* becomes *halves,* and *knife* becomes *knives.*

Some exceptions are *roof/roofs* and *reef/reefs.*

Nouns Ending in o

When forming plurals with nouns ending in a consonant and *o,* the *o* is kept and an *es* is added. For example, *tomato* becomes *tomatoes.*

Musical terms are the exception to this rule. Words like *soprano* and *piano* are pluralized by adding *s* even though they end in a consonant and *o* (*sopranos, pianos*).

When forming plurals with nouns ending in a vowel and *o,* the *o* is kept, and *s* is added. For example, *ratio* becomes *ratios,* and *patio* becomes *patios.*

Exceptions to the Rules of Plurals

For some nouns, instead of changing or adding letters at the end of the word, changes to the vowels *within* the words are necessary. For example:

- *man* becomes *men*
- woman becomes women
- child becomes children

Some nouns, when pluralized, change entirely:

- tooth becomes teeth
- *foot* becomes *feet*
- *mouse* becomes *mice*

The opposite is also true; some nouns are the same in the plural as they are in the singular form. For example, *deer, species, fish,* and *sheep* are all plural nouns in singular form.

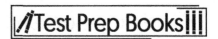

Practice Questions

Directions: In the following sentences, choose the correct spelling of the missing word. Mark the letter that identifies your choice on the answer sheet.

1. A non-violent breach of a law to bring about social change is called civil _____.
    a. disobidiance.
    b. disobedense.
    c. disobedience.
    d. disobediance.

2. After graduating from the Police Academy, you will be assigned to a _____.
    a. pricinct.
    b. precint.
    c. precinct.
    d. presinct.

3. Becoming a police officer is a great _____ to serve your community.
    a. oppurtinity
    b. opportunity
    c. opportinity
    d. oppurtunity

4. I _____ spilled coffee on my desk.
    a. acidentally
    b. assidentilly
    c. accidentilly
    d. accidentally

5. Your excellent work shows how _____ you are to the job.
    a. comited
    b. comitted
    c. commited
    d. committed

6. My flushed cheeks gave away my _____.
    a. embarassmint.
    b. embarrasment.
    c. embarrissment.
    d. embarrassment.

7. We have the lowest price, _____.
    a. guarenteed.
    b. guaranted.
    c. guarinteed.
    d. guaranteed.

8. Though baseball is my favorite sport, I _____ play golf.
   a. occasionaly
   b. occasionally
   c. ocassionally
   d. occassionaly

9. The *New York Journal* has _____ endorsed Andrew Walter for Congress.
   a. explicitally
   b. explicitly
   c. explicitely
   d. explicately

10. A _____ approach to cooking will ensure that your meals are healthy and delicious.
   a. conscientios
   b. conciencious
   c. conscientious
   d. consciencious

11. I'm _____ looking forward to my vacation this year.
   a. definitly
   b. definitely
   c. defenitely
   d. definately

12. I hope that scientists are able to prove the _____ of aliens.
   a. existanse
   b. esixtinse
   c. existense
   d. existence

13. _____ speaking, our operating system is one of the best on the market.
   a. Technicaly
   b. Technicilly
   c. Technically
   d. Technikcally

14. When in need of advice on a case, I consult with my _____.
   a. sergeant.
   b. sergant.
   c. saergant.
   d. seargeant.

15. The car was _____ new when she purchased it.
   a. practicilly
   b. practicaly
   c. practikally
   d. practically

Answer Explanations

1. C

2. C

3. B

4. D

5. D

6. D

7. D

8. B

9. B

10. C

11. B

12. D

13. C

14. A

15. D

Vocabulary

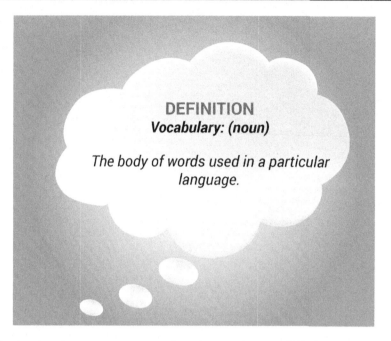

DEFINITION
Vocabulary: (noun)

The body of words used in a particular language.

Vocabulary is simply the words a person uses and understands on a daily basis. Having a good vocabulary is important in both written and verbal communications. In law enforcement, officers may have to read court records, police reports, and other legal documents. Many of these materials may contain unfamiliar words, so it's important for officers to learn ways to uncover a word's meaning so they can use it correctly in their own writing.

To understand the challenges of using vocabulary correctly, imagine suddenly being thrust into a foreign country. Not knowing the right words to use when asking for basic necessities (e.g., food, a place to stay, a bathroom) would make everyday life extremely difficult. Asking for help from foreigners who don't share the same vocabulary is hard, since language is what facilitates understanding between people. The more vocabulary words a person understands, the more precisely they can communicate their intentions. This section of the study guide focuses on understanding and deciphering vocabulary through basic grammar.

Prefixes and Suffixes

In the previous section, we went over the particular *spelling* of prefixes and suffixes, and how they changed the root word. In this section, we will look at the *meaning* of various prefixes and suffixes when added to a root word. As mentioned before, a *prefix* is a combination of letters found at the beginning of a word, while a *suffix* is a combination of letters found at the end. A *root word* is the word that comes after the prefix, before the suffix, or between them both. Sometimes a root word can stand on its own without either a prefix or a suffix. More simply put:

Prefix + Root Word = Word

Root Word + Suffix = Word

Prefix + Root Word + Suffix = Word

Root Word = Word

Knowing the definitions of common prefixes and suffixes can help when trying to determine the meaning of an unknown word. In addition, knowing prefixes can help in determining the number of things, the negative of something, or the time and space of an object. Understanding suffix definitions can help when trying to determine the meaning of an adjective, noun, or verb.

The following charts review some of the most common prefixes, what they mean, and how they're used to decipher a word's meaning:

Number and Quantity Prefixes

Prefix	Definition	Example
bi-	two	bicycle, bilateral
mono-	one, single	monopoly, monotone
poly-	many	polygamy, polygon
semi-	half, partly	semiannual, semicircle
uni-	one	unicycle, universal

Here's an example of a number prefix:

The countries signed a *bilateral* agreement; both had to abide by the contract.

Look at the word *bilateral*. If the root word (*lateral*) is unfamiliar, the prefix (*bi-*) can provide a vital clue to its meaning. The prefix *bi-* means *two*, which shows that the agreement involves two of something, most likely the two countries, since *both had to abide by the contract*. This is correct since *bilateral* actually means "involving two parties, usually countries."

Negative Prefixes

Prefix	Definition	Example
a-	without, lack of	amoral, atypical
in-	not, opposing	inability, inverted
non-	not	nonexistent, nonstop
un-	not, reverse	unable, unspoken

Here's an example of a negative prefix:

The patient's *inability* to speak made the doctor wonder what was wrong.

Look at the word *inability*. In the chart above, the prefix *in-* means *not* or *opposing*. By replacing the prefix with *not* and placing it in front of the root word of *ability* (*able*), the meaning of the word becomes clear: *not able*. Therefore, the patient was *not able* to speak.

Time and Space Prefixes

Prefix	Definition	Example
a-	in, on, of, up, to	aloof, associate
ab-	from, away, off	abstract, absent
ad-	to, towards	adept, adjacent
ante-	before, previous	antebellum, antenna
anti-	against, opposing	anticipate, antisocial
cata-	down, away, thoroughly	catacomb, catalogue
circum-	around	circumstance, circumvent
com-	with, together, very	combine, compel
contra-	against, opposing	contraband, contrast
de-	from	decrease, descend
dia-	through, across, apart	diagram, dialect
dis-	away, off, down, not	disregard, disrespect
epi-	upon	epidemic, epiphany
ex-	out	example, exit
hypo-	under, beneath	hypoallergenic, hypothermia
inter-	among, between	intermediate, international
intra-	within	intrapersonal, intravenous
ob-	against, opposing	obtain, obscure
per-	through	permanent, persist
peri-	around	periodontal, periphery
post-	after, following	postdate, postoperative
pre-	before, previous	precede, premeditate
pro-	forward, in place of	program, propel
retro-	back, backward	retroactive, retrofit
sub-	under, beneath	submarine, substantial
super-	above, extra	superior, supersede
trans-	across, beyond, over	transform, transmit
ultra-	beyond, excessively	ultraclean, ultralight

Here's an example of a space prefix:

The teacher's motivational speech helped *propel* her students toward greater academic achievement.

Look at the word *propel*. The prefix *pro-* means *forward* or *in place of* which indicates something relevant to time and space. *Propel* means to drive or move in a direction (usually forward), so knowing the prefix *pro-* helps interpret that the students are moving forward *toward greater academic achievement*.

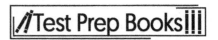

Miscellaneous Prefixes

Prefix	Definition	Example
belli-	war, warlike	bellied, belligerent
bene-	well, good	benediction, beneficial
equi-	equal	equidistant, equinox
for-	away, off, from	forbidden, forsaken
fore-	previous	forecast, forebode
homo-	same, equal	homogeneous, homonym
hyper-	excessive, over	hyperextend, hyperactive
in-	in, into	insignificant, invasive
magn-	large	magnetic, magnificent
mal-	bad, poorly, not	maladapted, malnourished
mis-	bad, poorly, not	misplace, misguide
mor-	death	mortal, morgue
neo-	new	neoclassical, neonatal
omni-	all, everywhere	omnipotent, omnipresent
ortho-	right, straight	orthodontist, orthopedic
over-	above	overload, overstock,
pan-	all, entire	panacea, pander
para-	beside, beyond	paradigm, parameter
phil-	love, like	philanthropy, philosophic
prim-	first, early	primal, primer
re-	backward, again	reload, regress
sym-	with, together	symmetry, symbolize
vis-	to see	visual, visibility

Here's another prefix example:

The computer was *primitive*; it still had a floppy disk drive!

The word *primitive* has the prefix *prim-* which indicates being *first* or *early*. *Primitive* means the historical development of something. Therefore, the sentence infers that the computer is an older model because it no longer has a floppy disk drive.

The charts that follow review some of the most common suffixes and include examples of how they're used to determine the meaning of a word. Remember, suffixes are added to the *end* of a root word:

Adjective Suffixes

Suffix	Definition	Example
-able (-ible)	capable of being	teachable, accessible
-esque	in the style of, like	humoresque, statuesque
-ful	filled with, marked by	helpful, deceitful
-ic	having, containing	manic, elastic
-ish	suggesting, like	malnourish, tarnish
-less	lacking, without	worthless, fearless
-ous	marked by, given to	generous, previous

Here's an example of an adjective suffix:

The live model looked so *statuesque* in the window display; she didn't even move!

Look at the word *statuesque*. The suffix *-esque* means *in the style of* or *like*. If something is *statuesque*, it's *in the style of a statue* or *like a statue*. In this sentence, the model looks *like* a statue.

Noun Suffixes

Suffix	Definition	Example
-acy	state, condition	literacy, legacy
-ance	act, condition, fact	distance, importance
-ard	one that does	leotard, billiard
-ation	action, state, result	legislation, condemnation
-dom	state, rank, condition	freedom, kingdom
-er (-or)	office, action	commuter, spectator
-ess	feminine	caress, princess
-hood	state, condition	childhood, livelihood
-ion	action, result, state	communion, position
-ism	act, manner, doctrine	capitalism, patriotism
-ist	worker, follower	stylist, activist
-ity (-ty)	state, quality, condition	community, dirty
-ment	result, action	empowerment, segment
-ness	quality, state	fitness, rudeness
-ship	position	censorship, leadership
-sion (-tion)	state, result	tension, transition
-th	act, state, quality	twentieth, wealth
-tude	quality, state, result	attitude, latitude

Look at the following example of a noun suffix:

The *spectator* cheered when his favorite soccer team scored a goal.

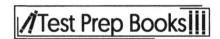

Look at the word *spectator*. The suffix *-or* means *action*. In this sentence, the *action* is to *spectate* (watch something), thus a *spectator* is someone involved in watching something.

Verb Suffixes

Suffix	Definition	Example
-ate	having, showing	facilitate, integrate
-en	cause to be, become	frozen, written
-fy	make, cause to have	modify, rectify
-ize	cause to be, treat with	realize, sanitize

Here's an example of a verb suffix:

> The preschool had to *sanitize* the toys every Tuesday and Thursday.

In the word *sanitize*, the suffix *-ize* means *cause to be* or *treat with*. By adding the suffix *-ize* to the root word *sanitary*, the meaning of the word becomes active: *cause to be sanitary*.

Context Clues

It's common to encounter unfamiliar words in written communication. When faced with an unknown word, there are certain "tricks" that can be used to uncover its meaning. *Context clues* are words or phrases within a sentence or paragraph that provide hints about a word and its definition. For example, if an unfamiliar word is anchored to a noun with other attached words as clues, these can help decipher the word's meaning. Consider the following example:

> After the treatment, Grandma's natural rosy cheeks looked *wan* and ghostlike.

The unfamiliar word is *wan*. The first clue to its meaning is in the phrase *After the treatment,* which implies that something happened after a procedure (possibly medical). A second clue is the word *rosy*, which describes Grandma's natural cheek color that changed after the treatment. Finally, the word *ghostlike* infers that Grandma's cheeks now look white. By using the context clues in the sentence, the meaning of the word *wan* (which means *pale*) can be deciphered.

Below are some additional ways to use context clues to uncover the meaning of an unknown word:

Contrasts

Look for context clues that *contrast* the unknown word. When reading a sentence with an unfamiliar word, look for a contrasting or opposing word or idea. Here's an example:

> Since Mary didn't cite her research sources, she lost significant points for *plagiarizing* the content of her report.

In this sentence, *plagiarizing* is the unfamiliar word. Notice that when Mary *didn't cite her research sources,* it resulted in her losing points for *plagiarizing the content of her report*. These contrasting ideas infer that Mary did something wrong with the content. This makes sense because the definition of *plagiarizing* is "taking the work of someone else and passing it off as your own."

Contrasts often use words like *but, however, although,* or phrases like *on the other hand.* For example:

The *gargantuan* television won't fit in my car, but it will cover the entire wall in the den.

The unfamiliar word is *gargantuan.* Notice that the television is too big to fit in a car, <u>*but it will cover the entire wall in the den*</u>. This infers that the television is extremely large, which is correct, since the word *gargantuan* means "enormous."

Synonyms
Another method is to brainstorm possible synonyms for the unknown word. *Synonyms* are words with the same or similar meanings (e.g., *strong* and *sturdy*). To do this, substitute synonyms one at a time, reading the sentence after each to see if the meaning is clear. By replacing an unknown word with a known one, it may be possible to uncover its meaning. For example:

Gary's clothes were *saturated* after he fell into the swimming pool.

In this sentence, the word *saturated* is unknown. To brainstorm synonyms for *saturated*, think about what happens to Gary's clothes after falling into the swimming pool. They'd be *soaked* or *wet*, both of which turn out to be good synonyms to try since the actual meaning of *saturated* is "thoroughly soaked."

Antonyms
Sometimes sentences contain words or phrases that oppose each other. Opposite words are known as *antonyms* (e.g., *hot* and *cold*). For example:

Although Mark seemed *tranquil,* you could tell he was actually nervous as he paced up and down the hall.

The unknown word here is *tranquil.* The sentence says that Mark was in fact not *tranquil* but was instead *actually nervous.* The opposite of the word *nervous* is *calm,* which is the meaning of the word *tranquil.*

Explanations or Descriptions
Explanations or *descriptions* of other things in the sentence can also provide clues to an unfamiliar word. Take the following example:

Golden Retrievers, Great Danes, and Pugs are the top three *breeds* competing in the dog show.

If the word *breeds* is unknown, look at the sentence for an explanation or description that provides a clue. The subjects (*Golden Retrievers, Great Danes*, and *Pugs*) describe different types of dogs. This description helps uncover the meaning of the word *breeds* which is "a particular type or group of animals."

Inferences
Sometimes there are clues to an unknown word that infer or suggest its meaning. These *inferences* can be found either within the sentence where the word appears or in a sentence that precedes or follows it. Look at the following example:

The *wretched* old lady was kicked out of the restaurant. She was so mean and nasty to the waiter!

Here the word *wretched* is unknown. The first sentence states that the *old lady was kicked out of the restaurant*, but it doesn't say why. The sentence that follows tells us why: *She was so mean and nasty to the waiter!* This infers that the old lady was *kicked out* because she was *so mean and nasty* or, in other words, *wretched*.

When preparing for a vocabulary test, try reading challenging materials to learn new words. If a word on the test is unfamiliar, look for prefixes and suffixes to help uncover what the word means and eliminate incorrect answers. If two answers both seem right, determine if there are any differences between them and then select the word that best fits. Context clues in the sentence or paragraph can also help to uncover the meaning of an unknown word. By learning new vocabulary words, a person can expand their knowledge base and improve the quality and effectiveness of their written communications.

Practice Questions

Directions: Read each sentence carefully and select the answer that is closest in meaning to the underlined word. Use prefix/suffix definitions and context clues to help eliminate incorrect answers.

1. Only one of the thieves who robbed the jewelry store was caught since his <u>accomplice</u> got away.
    a. Roommate
    b. Brother
    c. Partner
    d. Manager

2. The congressman denied the <u>allegation</u> that he'd voted in favor of the bill in exchange for a campaign donation.
    a. Claim
    b. Reptile
    c. Highway
    d. Interrogation

3. During the <u>arraignment</u> in front of the judge, Tommy pleaded not guilty to driving under the influence of alcohol.
    a. Wedding
    b. Proceeding
    c. Bouquet
    d. Conclusion

4. The violent offender was convicted of <u>battery</u> for using a baseball bat to strike his victim.
    a. Voltage
    b. Assault
    c. Flattery
    d. Arson

5. The gang members in Shelly's neighborhood tried to <u>coerce</u> her into selling drugs, but she refused to be bullied.
    a. Pay
    b. Discourage
    c. Gender
    d. Pressure

6. The company treasurer was found guilty of <u>embezzling</u> $50,000 from the company's bank account to pay for the remodeling of his home.
    a. Bedazzling
    b. Stealing
    c. Decorating
    d. Borrowing

7. The judge <u>exonerated</u> Susan of all charges, so she left the courtroom a free woman.
   a. Cleared
   b. Executed
   c. Tried
   d. Convicted

8. When officers arrived on the scene of the deadly crash, they learned there had been one <u>fatality</u>.
   a. Birth
   b. Attraction
   c. Death
   d. Celebration

9. The unsuspecting art collector didn't realize the painting was a <u>forgery</u> until after it was appraised, so she became the 13th victim of the con artist.
   a. Antique
   b. Operation
   c. Sculpture
   d. Fake

10. The criminals wore gloves so they wouldn't leave behind any <u>latent</u> fingerprints.
    a. Hidden
    b. Painted
    c. Vinyl
    d. Visible

11. The state declared a <u>moratorium</u> on executions after new evidence cleared one death row inmate of his crime.
    a. Funeral
    b. Postponement
    c. Speech
    d. Hospitalization

12. The witness said the <u>perpetrator</u> wore a black ski mask and a blonde wig during the home invasion.
    a. Model
    b. Student
    c. Criminal
    d. Dancer

13. Though Miss Johnson swore to tell the truth under oath, she actually tried to <u>prevaricate</u> and claimed she didn't remember any details.
    a. Steal
    b. Impregnate
    c. Lie
    d. Confess

14. The city's first responders must follow <u>protocol</u> when handling calls for cases of domestic violence.
    a. Guidelines
    b. Internist
    c. Requests
    d. Evidence

15. After the riot broke out, officers had to use strong measures to <u>quell</u> the angry crowd.
    a. Wave
    b. Count
    c. Incite
    d. Calm

Answer Explanations

1. C: *Partner*: a person who takes part in a plan with another or other persons

Accomplice: a person who joins another person in the act of carrying out a plan (most likely an illegal or unethical one)

2. A: *Claim*: a declaration that something is the truth without the accompaniment of evidence

Allegation: a claim or assertion of some wrongdoing, typically made without proof

3. B: *Proceeding*: the steps of carrying out the law within an institution

Arraignment: the courtroom proceeding where a defendant is apprised of the charges against them and enters a plea of guilty or not guilty

4. B: *Assault*: to attack suddenly and unlawfully

Battery: an assault where the assailant makes physical contact with another person

5. D: *Pressure*: to influence someone to do a particular thing

Coerce: to persuade an unwilling person to do something by using pressure, intimidation, or threats

6. B: *Stealing*: the act of taking a thing from somebody that isn't one's own

Embezzling: to defraud someone or to steal property (often money) entrusted into one's care

7. A: *Cleared*: to be absolved of misunderstanding or doubt

Exonerated: to be pronounced not guilty of criminal charges

8. C: *Death*: the event of a person's life ending

Fatality: a death that occurs as the result of an accident, disaster, war, or disease

9. D: *Fake*: an imitation of reality; a simulation

Forgery: to create or imitate something (e.g., an object or document) with the intent to deceive others or profit from the sale of it

10. A: *Hidden*: something kept out of sight or concealed

Latent: a thing that's hidden, or something that exists but hasn't been developed yet

11. B: *Postponement*: to hold off on a scheduled activity until a later date

Moratorium: a legal postponement or waiting period set by some authority to suspend activity

12. C: *Criminal*: someone who is guilty of a crime

Perpetrator: the person who commits a crime

13. C: *Lie*: to state a contradiction of the truth; to deceive

Prevaricate: to deliberately evade the truth or lie in order to mislead

14. A: *Guidelines*: a set of standards created for a future action

Protocol: official guidelines or procedures that must be followed

15. D: *Calm*: to make tranquil or serene

Quell: to calm, quiet, or put an end to something

Reading Comprehension

Types of Passages

Writing can be classified under four passage types: narrative, expository, descriptive (sometimes called technical), and persuasive. Though these types are not mutually exclusive, one form tends to dominate the rest. By recognizing the *type* of passage you're reading, you gain insight into *how* you should read. If you're reading a narrative, you can assume the author intends to entertain, which means you may skim the text without losing meaning. A technical document might require a close read, because skimming the passage might cause the reader to miss salient details.

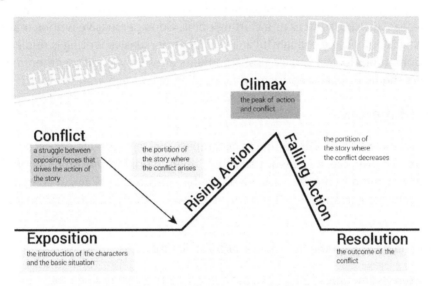

1. *Narrative* writing, at its core, is the art of storytelling. For a narrative to exist, certain elements must be present. First, it must have characters While many characters are human, characters could be defined as anything that thinks, acts, and talks like a human. For example, many recent movies, such as *Lord of the Rings* and *The Chronicles of Narnia*, include animals, fantastical creatures, and even trees that behave like humans. Second, it must have a plot or sequence of events. Typically, those events follow a standard plot diagram, but recent trends start *in medias res* or in the middle (near the climax). In this instance, foreshadowing and flashbacks often fill in plot details. Finally, along with characters and a plot, there must also be conflict. Conflict is usually divided into two types: internal and external. Internal conflict indicates the character is in turmoil and is presented through the character's thoughts. External conflicts are visible. Types of external conflict include person versus person, person versus nature, person versus technology, person versus the supernatural, or a person versus fate.

2. *Expository writing is detached and to the point. Since expository* writing is designed to instruct or inform, it usually involves directions and steps written in second person ("you" voice) and lacks any persuasive or narrative elements. Sequence words such as *first, second*, and *third*, or *in the first place, secondly*, and *lastly* are often given to add fluency and cohesion. Common examples of expository writing include instructor's lessons, cookbook recipes, and repair manuals.

3. Due to its empirical nature, *technical* writing is filled with steps, charts, graphs, data, and statistics. The goal of technical writing is to advance understanding in a field through the scientific method.

Experts such as teachers, doctors, or mechanics use words unique to the profession in which they operate. These words, which often incorporate acronyms, are called *jargon*. Technical writing is a type of expository writing but is not meant to be understood by the general public. Instead, technical writers assume readers have received a formal education in a particular field of study and need no explanation as to what the jargon means. Imagine a doctor trying to understand a diagnostic reading for a car or a mechanic trying to interpret lab results. Only professionals with proper training will fully comprehend the text.

4. *Persuasive* writing is designed to change opinions and attitudes. The topic, stance, and arguments are found in the thesis, positioned near the end of the introduction. Later supporting paragraphs offer relevant quotations, paraphrases, and summaries from primary or secondary sources, which are then interpreted, analyzed, and evaluated. The goal of persuasive writers is not to stack quotes, but to develop original ideas by using sources as a starting point. Good persuasive writing makes powerful arguments with valid sources and thoughtful analysis. Poor persuasive writing is riddled with bias and logical fallacies. Sometimes logical and illogical arguments are sandwiched together in the same text. Therefore, readers should display skepticism when reading persuasive arguments.

Organization of the Text

Depending on what the author is attempting to accomplish, certain formats or text structures work better than others. For example, a sequence structure might work for narration but not when identifying similarities and differences between dissimilar concepts. Similarly, a comparison-contrast structure is not useful for narration. It's the author's job to put the right information in the correct format.

Readers should be familiar with the five main literary structures:

1. *Sequence* structure (sometimes referred to as the order structure) is when the order of events proceeds in a predictable order. In many cases, this means the text goes through the plot elements: exposition, rising action, climax, falling action, and resolution. Readers are introduced to characters, setting, and conflict in the exposition. In the rising action, there's an increase in tension and suspense. The climax is the height of tension and the point of no return. Tension decreases during the falling action. In the resolution, any conflicts presented in the exposition are resolved, and the story concludes. An informative text that is structured sequentially will often go in order from one step to the next.

2. In the *problem-solution* structure, authors identify a potential problem and suggest a solution. This form of writing is usually divided into two paragraphs and can be found in informational texts. For example, cell phone, cable, and satellite providers use this structure in manuals to help customers troubleshoot or identify problems with services or products.

3. When authors want to discuss similarities and differences between separate concepts, they arrange thoughts in a *comparison-contrast* paragraph structure. Venn diagrams are an effective graphic organizer for comparison-contrast structures, because they feature two overlapping circles that can be used to organize similarities and differences. A comparison-contrast essay organizes one paragraph based on similarities and another based on differences. A comparison-contrast essay can also be arranged with the similarities and differences of individual traits addressed within individual paragraphs. Words such as *however*, *but*, and *nevertheless* help signal a contrast in ideas.

4. *Descriptive* writing structure is designed to appeal to your senses. Much like an artist who constructs a painting, good descriptive writing builds an image in the reader's mind by appealing to the five senses:

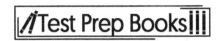

sight, hearing, taste, touch, and smell. However, overly descriptive writing can become tedious; likewise, sparse descriptions can make settings and characters seem flat. Good authors strike a balance by applying descriptions only to passages, characters, and settings that are integral to the plot.

5. Passages that use the *cause and effect* structure are simply asking *why* by demonstrating some type of connection between ideas. Words such as *if, since, because, then,* or *consequently* indicate relationship. By switching the order of a complex sentence, the writer can rearrange the emphasis on different clauses. Saying *If Sheryl is late, we'll miss the dance* is different from saying *We'll miss the dance if Sheryl is late.* One emphasizes Sheryl's tardiness while the other emphasizes missing the dance. Paragraphs can also be arranged in a cause and effect format. Since the format—before and after—is sequential, it is useful when authors wish to discuss the impact of choices. Researchers often apply this paragraph structure to the scientific method.

Purposes for Writing

When it comes to authors' writings, readers should always identify a position or stance. No matter how objective a text may seem, assume the author has preconceived beliefs. Reduce the likelihood of accepting an invalid argument by looking for multiple articles on the topic, including those with varying opinions. If several opinions point in the same direction, and are backed by reputable peer-reviewed sources, it's more likely the author has a valid argument. Positions that run contrary to widely held beliefs and existing data should invite scrutiny. There are exceptions to the rule, so be a careful consumer of information. Though themes, symbols, and motifs are buried deep within the text and can sometimes be difficult to infer, an author's purpose is usually obvious from the beginning.

No matter the genre or format, authors write to persuade, inform, entertain, or express feelings. Often, these purposes are blended, with one dominating the rest. It's useful to learn to recognize the author's intent.

As mentioned before in the *Types of Passages* section, authors use persuasive writing to convince readers of something. It often contains two elements: the argument and the counterargument. The argument takes a stance on an issue, while the counterargument pokes holes in the opposition's stance. Authors rely on logic (logos), emotion (pathos), and credibility (ethos) to persuade readers to agree with them. If readers are opposed to the stance before reading, they are unlikely to adopt that stance. Those who are undecided or committed to the same stance are more likely to agree with the author.

Authors use informative writing to teach or inform. Informative writing includes technical writing or expository writing, as detailed before. Workplace manuals, instructor lessons, statistical reports and cookbooks are examples of informative texts. Informative writing is usually based on facts and is often void of emotion or persuasion. Informative texts likely contain statistics, charts, and graphs. Though most informative texts lack a persuasive agenda, readers must examine the text carefully to determine whether one exists within a given passage.

Authors use stories or narratives with the intent to entertain. When you go to the movies, you often want to escape for a few hours, not necessarily to think critically. Entertaining writing is designed to delight and engage the reader. However, sometimes this type of writing can be woven into more serious material, such as persuasive or informative writing, to hook the reader before transitioning into a more scholarly discussion.

Finally, emotional writing works to evoke the reader's feelings, such as anger, euphoria, or sadness. The connection between reader and author is an attempt to cause the reader to share the author's intended emotion or tone. Sometimes, the author simply wants readers to feel what they felt in order to make the text more poignant. Other times, the author attempts to persuade or manipulate the reader into adopting their stance. While it's okay to sympathize with the author, be aware of the individual's underlying intent.

Writing Devices

Authors utilize a wide range of devices to tell a story or communicate information. Readers should be familiar with the most common of these devices. Writing devices are also commonly known as *techniques of writing* or *rhetorical devices*.

Types of Appeals

In non-fiction writing, authors employ argumentative techniques to present their opinion to readers in the most convincing way. First of all, persuasive writing usually includes at least one type of appeal: an appeal to logic (logos), emotion (pathos), or credibility and trustworthiness (ethos). When a writer appeals to logic, they are asking readers to agree with them based on research, evidence, and an established line of reasoning. An author's argument might also appeal to readers' emotions, perhaps by including personal stories and anecdotes (a short narrative of a specific event). A final type of appeal, appeal to authority, asks the reader to agree with the author's argument on the basis of their expertise or credentials. Consider three different approaches to arguing the same opinion:

Logic (Logos)

> Our school should abolish its current ban on cell phone use on campus. This rule was adopted last year as an attempt to reduce class disruptions and help students focus more on their lessons. However, since the rule was enacted, there has been no change in the number of disciplinary problems in class. Therefore, the rule is ineffective and should be done away with.

The above is an example of an appeal to logic. The author uses evidence to disprove the logic of the school's rule (the rule was supposed to reduce discipline problems; the number of problems has not been reduced; therefore, the rule is not working) and call for its repeal.

Emotion (Pathos)

An author's argument might also appeal to readers' emotions, perhaps by including personal stories and anecdotes.

The next example presents an appeal to emotion. By sharing the personal anecdote of one student and speaking about emotional topics like family relationships, the author invokes the reader's empathy in asking them to reconsider the school rule.

> Our school should abolish its current ban on cell phone use on campus. If they aren't able to use their phones during the school day, many students feel isolated from their loved ones. For example, last semester, one student's grandmother had a heart attack in the morning. However, because he couldn't use his cell phone, the student didn't know about his grandmother's accident until the end of the day—when she had already passed away, and it was too late to say goodbye. By preventing students from contacting their friends and family, our school is placing undue stress and anxiety on students.

Credibility (Ethos)

Finally, an appeal to authority includes a statement from a relevant expert. In this case, the author uses a doctor in the field of education to support the argument. All three examples begin from the same opinion—the school's phone ban needs to change—but rely on different argumentative styles to persuade the reader.

> Our school should abolish its current ban on cell phone use on campus. According to Dr. Bartholomew Everett, a leading educational expert, "Research studies show that cell phone usage has no real impact on student attentiveness. Rather, phones provide a valuable technological resource for learning. Schools need to learn how to integrate this new technology into their curriculum." Rather than banning phones altogether, our school should follow the advice of experts and allow students to use phones as part of their learning.

Rhetorical Questions

Another commonly used argumentative technique is asking rhetorical questions, questions that do not actually require an answer but that push the reader to consider the topic further.

> I wholly disagree with the proposal to ban restaurants from serving foods with high sugar and sodium contents. Do we really want to live in a world where the government can control what we eat? I prefer to make my own food choices.

Here, the author's rhetorical question prompts readers to put themselves in a hypothetical situation and imagine how they would feel about it.

Figurative Language

Simile and *metaphor* are part of figurative language and are used as rhetorical devices. Both are comparisons between two things, but their formats differ slightly. A simile says that two things are *similar* and makes a comparison using *like* or *as*—A is like B, or A is as [some characteristic] as B—whereas a metaphor states that two things are exactly the same—A is B. In both cases, simile and metaphor invite the reader to think more deeply about the characteristics of the two subjects and consider where they overlap. An example of a metaphor would be Shakespeare's line "Juliette is the sun," where Romeo compares Juliette's radiance directly to the sun. For an example of simile, look at the first line of Robert Burns' famous poem:

> My love is like a red, red rose

This is comparison using *like*, and the two things being compared are love and a rose. Some characteristics of a rose are that it is fragrant, beautiful, blossoming, colorful, vibrant—by comparing his love to a red, red rose, Burns asks the reader to apply these qualities of a rose to his love. In this way, he implies that his love is also fresh, blossoming, and brilliant.

Point of View

Point of view is an important writing device to consider. In fiction writing, point of view refers to who tells the story or from whose perspective readers are observing as they read. In non-fiction writing, the *point of view* refers to whether the author refers to themselves, the readers, or chooses not to mention either. Whether fiction or nonfiction, the author will carefully consider the impact the perspective will have on the purpose and main point of the writing.

- First-person point of view: The story is told from the writer's perspective. In fiction, this would mean that the main character is also the narrator. First-person point of view is easily recognized by the use of personal pronouns such as *I, me, we, us, our, my,* and *myself*.

- Third-person point of view: In a more formal essay, this would be an appropriate perspective because the focus should be on the subject matter, not the writer or the reader. Third-person point of view is recognized by the use of the pronouns *he, she, they,* and *it*. In fiction writing, third person point of view has a few variations.

  - *Third-person limited* point of view refers to a story told by a narrator who has access to the thoughts and feelings of just one character.

  - In *third-person omniscient* point of view, the narrator has access to the thoughts and feelings of all the characters.

  - In *third-person objective* point of view, the narrator is like a fly on the wall and can see and hear what the characters do and say but does not have access to their thoughts and feelings.

- Second-person point of view: This point of view isn't commonly used in fiction or non-fiction writing because it directly addresses the reader using the pronouns *you, your,* and *yourself*. Second-person perspective is more appropriate in direct communication, such as business letters or emails.

Point of View	Pronouns used
First person	I, me, we, us, our, my, myself
Second person	You, your, yourself
Third person	He, she, it, they

Understanding a Passage

In order to understand any text, readers first need to determine what the text is about. In non-fiction writing, the text's *topic* is the most general answer to the question, "What is the writer talking about?" The topic can generally be expressed in just a few words. For example, a passage might be about college education, moving to a new neighborhood, or dog breeds. These are all examples of topics. Slightly more specific information is found in the *main idea*. The main idea answers the question, "What does the writer want readers to know about the topic?" One article might be about the history of popular dog breeds; another article might tell how certain dog breeds are unfairly stereotyped. In both cases, the topic is the same—dog breeds—but the main ideas are quite different. Each writer has a distinct purpose for writing and a different set of details for what they want us to know *about* dog breeds. Whereas the topic can usually be expressed in just a few words, the main idea can be explained in a full sentence. When a writer expresses their main idea in one sentence, this is also known as a *thesis statement* or thesis sentence. If a writer uses a thesis statement, it can generally be found at the beginning of the passage. Finally, the most specific information in a text is in its *supporting details*. To go back to the example of dog breeds, an article about dog breed stereotyping might discuss a case study of pit bulls and provide statistics about how many dog attacks are caused by pit bulls versus other breeds. This specific information that supports the main idea is known as a text's supporting details.

In contrast to informative writing, literary texts contain *themes*. A theme is a very general way to describe the ideas and questions raised in a piece of literature. Like a topic, a theme can often be expressed in just one word or a few words. However, due to the complex nature of literature, most texts contain more than one theme. Some examples of literary themes include isolation, sacrifice, or vengeance. A text's theme might also explore the relationship between two contrasting ideas: ignorance versus knowledge, nature versus technology, science versus religion. From these examples, it should be apparent that a theme generally expresses a relatively broad and abstract idea about the text—so don't confuse a text's theme with its subject. Both theme and subject can answer the question, "What is the story about?" but the subject answers the question in a concrete way whereas the theme answers it in a more abstract way. For example, the subject of *Hamlet* is Hamlet's investigation of his father's murder (a concrete idea of what happens in the story). However, its themes—that is, the ideas explored through the story—include indecision and revenge (fundamental concepts that unite the events of the story). Because the theme is usually abstract, it might seem difficult to identify. Readers can ask themselves several questions as they read to get a better idea of the theme:

- What observations does the writer make about human behavior?
- How do the specific events of this story relate to society in general?
- What forces drive the characters' actions and decisions?
- How did characters change or what did they learn during the story?

Again, remember that the theme generally refers to "big picture" ideas about the story, rather than a specific description of the story's events.

Evaluating a Passage

Readers draw *conclusions* about what an author has presented. This helps them better understand what the writer has intended to communicate and whether they agree with what the author has offered. There are a few ways to determine a logical conclusion, but careful reading is the most important. It's helpful to read a passage a few times, noting details that seem important to the text. Sometimes, readers arrive at a conclusion that is different than what the writer intended or come up with more than one conclusion.

Textual evidence within the details helps readers draw a conclusion about a passage. *Textual evidence* refers to information—facts and examples that support the main point. Textual evidence will likely come from outside sources and can be in the form of quoted or paraphrased material. In order to draw a conclusion from evidence, it's important to examine the credibility and validity of that evidence as well as how (and if) it relates to the main idea.

If an author presents a differing opinion or a counterargument in order to refute it, the reader should consider how and why this information is being presented. It is meant to strengthen the original argument and shouldn't be confused with the author's intended conclusion, but it should also be considered in the reader's final evaluation.

Summarizing is an effective way to draw a conclusion from a passage. A summary is a shortened version of the original text, written by the reader in their own words. Focusing on the main points of the original text and including only the relevant details can help readers reach a conclusion. It's important to retain the original meaning of the passage.

Like summarizing, *paraphrasing* can also help a reader fully understand different parts of a text. Paraphrasing calls for the reader to take a small part of the passage and list or describe its main points. Paraphrasing is more than rewording the original passage, though. It should be written in the reader's own words, while still retaining the meaning of the original source. This will indicate an understanding of the original source, yet still help the reader expand on their interpretation.

Responding to a Passage

There are a few ways for readers to engage actively with the text, such as making inferences and predictions. An *inference*, as mentioned earlier, refers to a point that is implied (as opposed to directly stated) by the evidence presented:

> Bradley packed up all of the items from his desk in a box and said goodbye to his coworkers for the last time.

From this sentence, though it is not directly stated, readers can infer that Bradley is leaving his job. It's necessary to use inference in order to draw conclusions about the meaning of a passage. When making an inference about a passage, it's important to rely only on the information that is provided in the text itself. This helps readers ensure that their conclusions are valid.

Readers will also find themselves making predictions when reading a passage or paragraph. *Predictions* are guesses about what's going to happen next. This is a natural tendency, especially when reading a good story or watching a suspenseful movie. It's fun to try to figure out how it will end. Authors intentionally use suspenseful language and situations to keep readers interested:

> A cat darted across the street just as the car came careening around the curve.

One unfortunate prediction might be that the car will hit the cat. Of course, predictions aren't always accurate, so it's important to read carefully to the end of the text to determine the accuracy of predictions.

Readers should pay attention to the *sequence*, or the order in which details are laid out in the text, as this can be important to understanding its meaning as a whole. Writers will often use transitional words to help the reader understand the order of events and to stay on track. Words like *next, then, after*, and *finally* show that the order of events is important to the author. In some cases, the author omits these transitional words, and the sequence is implied. Authors may even purposely present the information out of order to make an impact or have an effect on the reader. An example might be when a narrative writer uses *flashback* to reveal information.

Drawing conclusions is also important when actively reading a passage. *Hedge phrases* such as *will, might, probably*, and *appear to be* are used by writers who want to cover their bases and make sure to show there are exceptions to their statements. *Absolute phrasing*, such as *always* and *never*, should be carefully considered as they are often incorrect.

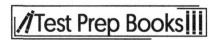

Critical Thinking Skills

It's important to read any text critically. The goal is to discover the point and purpose of what the author is writing about through analysis. It's also crucial to establish the point or stance the author has taken on the topic of the text. After determining the author's perspective, readers can then more effectively develop their own viewpoints on the subject of the text.

It is important to distinguish between *fact* and *opinion* when reading a text. When an author presents facts, such as statistics or data, readers should be able to check those facts and make sure they are accurate. When authors use opinion, they are sharing their own thoughts and feelings about a subject.

Authors often use words like *think, feel, believe,* or *in my opinion* when expressing opinion, but these words won't always appear in an opinion piece, especially if it is formally written. An author's opinion may be backed up by facts, which gives it more credibility, but that opinion should not be taken as fact. A critical reader should be suspect of an author's opinion, especially if it is only supported by other opinions.

Fact	Opinion
There are nine innings in a game of baseball.	Baseball games run too long.
James Garfield was assassinated on July 2, 1881.	James Garfield was a good president.
McDonalds has stores in 118 countries.	McDonalds has the best hamburgers.

Critical readers examine the facts used to support an author's argument. They check the facts against other sources to be sure those facts are correct. They also check the validity of the sources used to be sure those sources are credible, academic, and/or peer reviewed. Consider that when an author uses another person's opinion to support their argument, even if it is an expert's opinion, it is still only an opinion and should not be taken as fact. A strong argument uses valid, measurable facts to support ideas. Even then, the reader may disagree with the argument, as it may be rooted in personal beliefs.

An authoritative argument may use the facts to sway the reader. Take for example an argument about global warming. Many experts differ in their opinions of what alternative fuels can be used to aid in offsetting it. Because of this, a writer may choose to only use the information and expert opinion that supports their own viewpoint.

If the argument is that wind energy is the best solution, the author will use facts that support this idea. That same author may leave out relevant facts on solar energy. The way the author uses facts can influence the reader, so it's important to consider the facts being used, how those facts are being presented, and what information might be left out.

Critical readers should also look for errors in the argument such as logical fallacies and bias. A *logical fallacy* is a flaw in the logic used to make the argument. An example would be to rely on thinking that an event could potentially lead to a series of different, increasingly catastrophic events (*slippery slope fallacy*). For example, an author might want to assert that the obesity epidemic is the result of school lunch programs:

> School lunches don't offer healthy options. Kids eat these lunches every day, leading to weight gain. This weight gain can lead to obesity, so schools are to blame for the obesity epidemic.

This argument doesn't take into account the other factors that are at play here. Kids may not eat school lunch every day. It only accounts for one meal of the day for most kids. Even if the food is unhealthy, does the amount eaten factor in to weight gain? If the author can't prove with clear evidence that school lunches are actually leading to weight gain that the obesity epidemic stems from, their logic becomes mere speculation and is flawed.

Authors can also reflect *bias* if they ignore an opposing viewpoint or present their side in an unbalanced way. A strong argument considers the opposition and finds a way to refute it. Critical readers should look for an unfair or one-sided presentation of the argument and be skeptical, as a bias may be present. Even if this bias is unintentional, if it exists in the writing, the reader should be wary of the validity of the argument.

Readers should also look for the use of *stereotypes,* which refer to specific groups. Stereotypes are often negative connotations about a person or place and should always be avoided. When a critical reader finds stereotypes in a text, they should immediately be critical of the argument and consider the validity of anything the author presents. Stereotypes reveal a flaw in the writer's thinking and may suggest a lack of knowledge or understanding about the subject.

Practice Questions

Questions 1 and 2 are based on the following passage:

The majority of records that are taken as part of court proceedings are considered part of the public domain, and are therefore available to anyone who requests access. These documents can be used to conduct background checks, revealing information such as age, marital status, military status, and whether a person has ever been convicted of a crime. While many records are made public, some are sealed by a judge for extraordinary circumstances, such as to protect the privacy of a minor. Each state has its own rules governing which records can be accessed and counties determine how. In some cases the records can be obtained through a quick search of a state or county database, but others will require a request of the appropriate department. For example, in the state of California, most court records can be accessed through county court databases, but supreme and appellate court records are only available from the Appellate Court.

1. Based on the preceding passage, which of the following statements is most accurate?
   a. All court records can be accessed via online databases.
   b. Court records are always part of the public domain, so they can be accessed by anyone.
   c. Military status is private, so it cannot be revealed in court documents.
   d. For various reasons, some documents are sealed, so they are not accessible to the public.

2. Based on the preceding passage, which of the following statements is most accurate?
   a. Each state determines how and when court records can be accessed by the public.
   b. A judge should seal all court records for minors.
   c. A judge can seal a court record for any reason.
   d. California allows all court records to be accessed by county record databases.

Questions 3 and 4 are based on the following passage:

Conducting a traffic stop can be one of the most dangerous parts of being a police officer. In light of the many traffic stop incidents that have occurred all over the country, many states are looking at how to address the problem. Recently, the state of Illinois passed a new law that adds traffic stop training to their driver's education courses. These courses are aimed to make new drivers prepared for all the possibilities of the road, and a potential traffic stop by a police officer is one of those possibilities. Proponents of traffic stop training say that this could help new drivers, especially young teens, not to panic in the event they get pulled over. If they know what to expect and how to handle a traffic stop, it is hoped that they could protect themselves from doing anything that could be perceived as a threat, such as reaching under the seat or arguing with the officer. As this new driver's education component gains popularity, it could be seen in more states across the US, and hopefully reduce the amount of traffic stop incidents.

3. Based on the preceding passage, which of the following statements is most accurate?
   a. A new law in Illinois makes it required for all drivers to take driver's education courses.
   b. Lawmakers believe that traffic stop training will help police officers stop more underage drivers.
   c. Arguing with an officer is illegal during a traffic stop.
   d. The new law in Illinois adds traffic stop training to driver's education courses.

4. Based on the preceding passage, which of the following statements is most accurate?
   a. Traffic stops are not dangerous.
   b. Police officers can teach new drivers how to act when they are pulled over.
   c. Traffic stop training aims to protect young drivers from panicking when they are pulled over.
   d. Young drivers should not worry about being pulled over if they are driving safely.

Questions 5 and 6 are based on the following passage:

Federal law does not restrict the open carry of a weapon in public. Each state determines its own open carry laws. While there are some restrictions to these laws, such as having to gain a permit, or the prohibition of carrying a weapon in certain locations, such as a school or on public transportation, most states allow the open carry of a handgun. Currently, thirty-one states allow private citizens to open carry a firearm without a license. Only three states, California, Florida, and Illinois, and the District of Columbia, prohibit open carry of a firearm. Concealed carry refers to carrying a firearm under clothing or in a way that is not visible to the casual observer. Every state and the District of Columbia allow the concealed carry of a firearm in some form. Forty-two states do require a permit for concealed carry. Of these forty-two states, some have a "may issue" law that allows for wider denial of the permit and others have a "shall issue" law, which generally accepts most permits without discretion.

5. Based on the preceding passage, which of the following statements is most accurate?
   a. Open carry laws are strict in all fifty states.
   b. Only California, Florida, and Illinois allow for open carry of a firearm without a permit.
   c. Nineteen states require a permit for open carry of a firearm.
   d. Most states allow for open carry of a firearm with limited restrictions.

6. Based on the preceding passage, which of the following statements is most accurate?
   a. Eight states require a permit for concealed carry of a firearm in public.
   b. States that have a "may issue" law have very little restrictions on who can get a concealed carry permit.
   c. All states allow for the concealed carry of a firearm in public.
   d. States that have a "shall issue" law have strict restrictions on who can carry a weapon.

Questions 7 and 8 are based on the following passage:

Since the 1966 Supreme Court case, Miranda v. Arizona, police officers have been required to read the Miranda rights, or Miranda warning, to any person taken into police custody. The Miranda rights include the following:

- You have the right to remain silent.
- Anything you say can and will be used against you in a court of law.
- You have the right to an attorney.
- If you cannot afford an attorney, one will be appointed for you.

To fully comply with Miranda rights, the person in custody must also waive their rights, typically in writing. If they do not waive their rights, any information they provide is not admissible in court. Police officers are required to read these rights so that the person in custody is aware of them, but also to protect the information that is given in any questioning they might conduct. When a person in custody is not Mirandized, anything they say, such as a confession, or the location of evidence, cannot be used in court.

7. Based on the preceding passage, which of the following statements is most accurate?
   a. The Miranda rights require the person in custody to remain silent.
   b. The Miranda rights are the result of a Supreme Court case.
   c. Police officers are not always required to read the Miranda rights to a person in custody.
   d. The Miranda rights tell the person in custody that they don't need a lawyer.

8. Based on the preceding passage, which of the following statements is most accurate?
   a. Miranda rights only protect the person in custody.
   b. Police officers who do not read Miranda rights to a person in custody can be sued.
   c. A person must waive their Miranda rights in order for the information they provide to be admissible in court.
   d. Any information gained from a person in custody who has not waived their Miranda rights can be used in court.

Questions 9 and 10 are based on the following passage:

Many police departments have begun using social media outlets such as Twitter, Facebook, and Instagram to their benefit. Police departments have found that the use of social media can be very helpful in identifying suspects, alerting the community to a possible threat, locating a missing person, and even gaining support for their organization. Social media is a two-way street, so police departments are also able to get valuable information and feedback from the communities they serve. Departments who use social media report that when their community feels like they have a forum to voice their opinion, it creates a sense of trust in the police. Departments that do opt to use social media should abide by some simple rules such as limiting the amount of information released, especially on ongoing cases, using appropriate language, and having a single point of contact to manage the sites for continuity. Social media can be a great asset to any police department if used appropriately.

9. Based on the preceding passage, which of the following statements is most accurate?
    a. Police departments should make a Facebook page, but avoid Twitter and Instagram.
    b. Social media has been helpful to police departments in identifying suspects and locating missing persons.
    c. Community trust is not built through the use of social media outlets.
    d. Social media can be helpful to police departments, but it is not used very often.

10. Based on the preceding passage, which of the following statements is most accurate?
    a. Police departments should try to use a single person to manage social media pages.
    b. Police departments should make full use of social media by revealing the details of ongoing cases.
    c. Social media is not beneficial in ongoing cases.
    d. Police departments that want to use social media should hire a consultant to set up their sites.

Questions 11 and 12 are based on the following passage:

A Drug Free School Zone indicates an area where drug offenses carry stricter penalties. This policy was created in the 1970s to deter citizens from committing drug crimes on or around school grounds. A Drug Free School Zone is part of federal law, but states can vary the penalties enforced on those who are convicted of drug-related violations near school campuses. What constitutes a Drug Free School Zone is determined by each jurisdiction, but typically includes school grounds, adjacent areas within 1000 feet, and school buses. Since the 1970s, all fifty states and Washington D.C. have adopted a Drug Free School Zone policy. More recently, some states have reduced the penalties, believing them to be too harsh for minor drug offenses that happened to occur near a school.

11. Based on the previous passage, which of the following statements best describes the purpose of a Drug Free School Zone?
    a. To help police locate and arrest students who are dealing drugs.
    b. To help school staff to locate and eliminate the use of drugs on campus.
    c. To deter people from committing drug-related crimes on and around schools.
    d. To eliminate the use of drugs on school buses.

12. Based on the previous passage, which of the following statements is most accurate?
    a. All fifty states have a 1000-foot zone around each school building that is designated as a Drug Free School Zone.
    b. The Drug Free School Zone enforces stricter penalties on those committed of drug-related offenses on or around school grounds.
    c. The Drug Free School Zone does not include school buses.
    d. Most states have abandoned the Drug Free School Zone policy because the penalties are too harsh.

Questions 13 and 14 are based on the following passage:

Any division of government (federal, state, local) can declare a state of emergency. A state of emergency means that the government has suspended the normal constitutional procedures. In this case, citizens may not have the same rights that they typically do, such as driving on public roadways or whether they can remain in their homes. A state of emergency is typically declared in the wake of a disaster. Disasters can include hurricanes, tornadoes, floods, snowstorms, wildfires, and issues of public health such as a flu outbreak. In the event of a major snowstorm, for example, a government can issue a state of emergency to clear roads for emergency responders and to keep citizens safely in their homes. Declaring a state of emergency can also allow a government to access the use of funds, personnel, equipment, and supplies that are reserved for such a situation.

13. Based on the previous passage, which of the following statements best describes a state of emergency?
    a. The government suspends normal constitutional operations.
    b. Curfews are imposed by the government.
    c. All citizens must remain in their homes.
    d. The government can remove all citizens' rights

14. Which of the following statements is most accurate based on the preceding passage?
    a. Declaring a state of emergency guarantees states will receive federal funding.
    b. Only state government can declare a state of emergency.
    c. Declaring a state of emergency allows the government to access reserved funding, personnel, and supplies.
    d. A state of emergency does not include issues of public health.

Questions 15 and 16 are based on the following passage:

In the event of a riot, police officers need to be prepared with the necessary gear to manage a large and potentially dangerous crowd. Front line riot police officers are equipped with helmets, riot shields, and body armor for protection. They also may carry gas masks in the event that tear gas is used to incapacitate or disperse a crowd. Riot police officers do have firearms, but less lethal methods of crowd management are preferred. Officers have traditionally used batons and whips to manage unruly crowds. In more recent years, police have begun using more effective methods such as tear gas, pepper spray, tasers, and rubber bullets.

15. The main idea of this passage is best stated with which of the following sentences?
    a. Riot police use gas masks for protection from tear gas and pepper spray.
    b. Violent crowds should always be incapacitated with tear gas.
    c. Batons and whips are not very good methods of crowd control.
    d. Riot police must be prepared with the necessary equipment to manage a dangerous crowd.

16. Which of the following statements is most accurate based on the preceding passage?
    a. Body armor, helmets, and riot shields are used to protect officers in the front line of a riot.
    b. Unruly crowds don't usually require tear gas or pepper spray.
    c. Police are free to use lethal methods to control a dangerous crowd.
    d. Rubber bullets are much less dangerous than regular bullets.

Questions 17 and 18 are based on the following passage:

K-9 officers are specially trained police officers that handle police dogs. Officers are typically required to have three to five years of patrol experience before applying to a K-9 position. In addition to their traditional training, K-9 officers are required to complete several weeks of official K-9 training to be certified. This training includes skills such as drug and explosive detection, dog handling, crowd control, and search and rescue techniques. Most police dogs live and work with their handlers, so a K-9 officer will be expected to care for his or her dog full time. Most police dogs have ten-year careers, so this is a long-term commitment between dog and officer.

17. Which of the following statements best identifies the main idea of the preceding passage?
    a. Police dogs live and work with their handlers.
    b. K-9 officers should be prepared for a long-term commitment when they apply for this position.
    c. There are several requirements to becoming a K-9 officer.
    d. Patrol experience is necessary to apply for a K-9 officer position.

18. Which of the following statements is most accurate, based on the preceding passage?
    a. K-9 training involves learning search and rescue techniques.
    b. Crowd control is not part of K-9 training.
    c. K-9 training can take up to ten years.
    d. Three to five years of dog training experience are required to become a K-9 officer.

Questions 19 and 20 are based on the following passage:

The Americans with Disabilities Act (ADA) was passed in 1990 to prohibit discrimination and to grant equal opportunity to those with disabilities in employment, transportation, communication, education, government services, and access to public places. In 2008, the ADA was amended to include a broader definition of the term "disability." Those who have physical or mental impairments that limit their lives in one or more major aspects can be considered disabled. This includes, but is not limited to, vision, speech, and hearing impairments, paralysis, intellectual disabilities such as mental retardation, mental illness, and chronic conditions such as epilepsy or multiple sclerosis. Temporary or naturally occurring conditions such as a broken limb, pregnancy, or the flu are not considered disabilities under this act.

19. Which of the following statements best defines the term *disability*?
    a. A physical or mental impairment that limits a major aspect of life.
    b. Vision, speech, and hearing impairments that prevent a person from working.
    c. Any illness that prevents a person from completing their daily tasks, such as the flu.
    d. Mental illnesses such as depression, anxiety, schizophrenia, and bipolar disorder.

20. Based on the passage, which of the following statements is most accurate?
    a. The ADA prevents discrimination, but does not protect equal opportunity for the disabled.
    b. Chronic conditions such as diabetes can be considered a disability if they affect at least one major aspect of a person's life.
    c. Those with a broken limb can apply for temporary handicapped tags.
    d. In 2008 the ADA made changes to what constitutes a major aspect of life.

Answer Explanations

1. D: Based on the passage, the most accurate statement is that some court records are sealed for reasons such as protecting the privacy of a minor involved in the case. While many court records can be accessed in online databases, some must be requested from a specific department such as the Appellate Court. The majority of court records are considered part of the public domain, but not all records are made public. Military status is part of court documents and can therefore be revealed through those records that are made part of the public domain.

2. A: Based on the passage, the most accurate statement is that each state makes its own laws about how and when court records can be accessed by the public. While a judge can seal a record for a minor, it is not required. Also, judges do have the power to seal a record, but this is usually only done in extraordinary circumstances. In California, only some court records are available through county databases. Appellate and Supreme Court records must be accessed through the Appellate Court.

3. D: Based on the passage, the new law discussed will add training in what to do at a traffic stop to driver's education courses in Illinois, so this is the best answer. The new law only adds this component to the courses; it does not require that all drivers take the course. The law does not target underage drivers, but aims to protect them from doing anything risky during a stop, so the goal is not to pull over more teens. While it is not advised that drivers reach under the seat or argue with the officer, it is not illegal. Drivers should know their rights and exercise them.

4. C: Based on the passage, the best answer is that traffic stop training is aimed to prevent drivers from panicking when they are pulled over. Traffic stops are actually one of the more dangerous parts of being a police officer. While a young driver may learn from a police officer during a traffic stop, the paragraph focuses more on how driver's education courses are being updated to instruct young drivers on how to handle a traffic stop. The paragraph is stressing a need for education in what to do during a traffic stop, so the last statement contradicts that point. A driver who believes he is driving safely could still be stopped.

5. D: This statement is the most accurate because the passage states that thirty-one states allow private citizens to open carry a firearm without a license. Thus, open carry laws are not very strict in all fifty states. California, Florida, and Illinois are singled out not because they allow open carry without a permit, but because they are the only states that prohibit open carry of a firearm. Because of these states' laws on open carry, the final statement about nineteen states requiring a permit cannot be true.

6. C: This is the most accurate statement because the passage asserts that all states including the District of Columbia allow for concealed carry of a firearm in public. The passage states that forty-two states, not eight, require a permit for concealed carry of a firearm in public. The "may issue" law allows states to pose more restrictions on who can be granted a concealed carry permit, while the "shall issue" law is much less restrictive.

7. B: The passage begins by stating the Miranda rights have been required since the 1966 Supreme Court case of Miranda v. Arizona, so this is the most accurate statement. The Miranda rights do not require the person in custody to remain silent, but notify them that they may remain silent if they choose to. Police officers must read the Miranda rights to any person in custody to protect the information they may get in interrogation. The Miranda rights tell the person in custody that they have the right to an attorney and that one will be provided to them if they cannot afford an attorney.

8. C: This statement is the most accurate because the passage states that in order to comply with Miranda rights, a person in custody must waive their rights. Miranda rights protect both the person in custody and the police. They also protect the admissibility of the information gained in any questioning. While police officers could be sued for any number of reasons, the passage does not make any indication that they could be sued for not reading a person in custody their Miranda rights. When a person has not waived their Miranda rights, the information they provide may not be admissible in court.

9. B: The passage indicates that police departments can successfully use social media to identify suspects and find missing persons. The passage does not deter police departments from using any social media outlet. Trust can be built with the community when they feel they have a voice through police social media sites. The passage states that the use of social media by police departments is actually growing in popularity.

10. A: Based on the passage, this statement is the most accurate because it calls for a single point of contact to manage the sites for continuity. The passage actually calls for police departments to limit details on ongoing cases, but it does not say it is not beneficial in these cases. For example, the paragraph states that social media can be helpful in identifying a suspect, which would be for an ongoing case. That does not mean they should reveal all the details of the crime or anything that might jeopardize the case. While some departments may opt to hire a consultant to set up their social media sites, nothing in the paragraph suggests that this is necessary.

11. C: Based on the passage, the best description of the purpose of a Drug Free School Zone is to deter citizens from committing drug related crimes on and around school campuses. Nothing in the passage suggests the law was created to help police identify students who are dealing drugs. The laws do not help schools identify drug use on campus; they only make penalties stricter for those who do. While a Drug Free School Zone may help deter drug use on school buses, this is not the primary purpose of the policy.

12. B: Based on the passage, the most accurate statement is that Drug Free School Zones enforce stricter penalties on those committing drug offenses on or near school grounds. While some states do enforce a 1000-foot zone around schools, the passage states that this is only typically the case, and is not the case for all fifty states. The Drug Free School Zone does include buses in most states. The passage notes that some states have reduced penalties in Drug Free School Zones, deeming them too harsh, but it does not say that most states have abandoned the policy.

13. A: The statement that best defines a state of emergency is the suspension of normal constitutional operation. While a curfew may be imposed when a state of emergency is declared, this is not always the case. Citizens may need to remain in their homes, but in the case of a hurricane or flood, evacuations may be necessary, so this answer is incorrect. While a government does have a right to alter citizens' rights in a state of emergency, it is to maintain their safety, and does not extend to all of their rights as citizens.

14. C: Based on the passage, the best answer is that a state of emergency allows the government access to reserved supplies, funding, and personnel. The passage does not suggest that a state of emergency will guarantee federal funding to any government. Local, state, and federal government can declare a state of emergency. The passage states that issues of public health can be addressed with a state of emergency declaration.

15. D: This statement best captures the main idea, or main point of the paragraph, which is to show the necessary equipment police officers must have to best manage a riot. While riot police do use gas masks for protection, this is too specific to be the main idea of the paragraph. The passage mentions tear gas, but does not suggest it is the best method to manage a crowd, so this is not the main focus of the paragraph. The passage does mention that better methods of crowd control than batons and whips have been used in recent years, but this is a supporting detail, and not the main idea of the passage.

16. A: This is the most accurate statement based on the passage, because it directly states that front line riot police use these methods of protection. The passage does not determine whether crowds typically require tear gas or pepper spray. The passage states that less lethal methods are preferred over lethal methods. While rubber bullets are less dangerous than regular bullets, this is not mentioned in the passage.

17. C: This answer best identifies the main idea of the passage, which is to detail the requirements of becoming a K-9 officer. Police dogs do typically live and work with their handlers, and this is a long-term commitment, but these answers represent supporting details of the passage, not the main idea. Patrol experience is typically a requirement of becoming a K-9 officer, but again this is a supporting detail, not the main idea of the passage.

18. A: This statement is the most accurate because the passage lists search and rescue techniques as one of the skills learned in K-9 officer training. According to the passage, crowd control is a skill learned in K-9 training. K-9 training takes several weeks, not ten years. K-9 officers are required to have three to five years of patrol experience, not dog training experience, based on the passage.

19. A: Based on the passage, this statement best defines the term *disability*, which is a physical or mental impairment that limits a person in at least one major aspect of life. While visual, speech, and hearing impairments can be considered disabilities, they are examples of a disability and not a comprehensive definition. Illnesses such as the flu are temporary and cannot be considered a disability, nor is this a definition for the term *disability*. While these mental illnesses may be considered disabilities, again they are examples, and not a comprehensive definition of the term *disability*.

20. B: This statement is most accurate because the passage states that chronic conditions can be considered a disability as long as they affect one major aspect of a person's life. The ADA prevents discrimination and also protects equal opportunity for the disabled. While it may be true that a person with a broken limb can apply for a temporary handicapped tag, the paragraph doesn't mention this, so it is not the most accurate statement based on the passage. The ADA was amended in 2008 to make a broader description of the term *disability*, not to change what constitutes a major aspect of life.

Cloze Test

The California POST will assess reading comprehension skills through a Cloze Test, an exercise that measures how well readers understand what they've read as they read it. Test-takers will be given a passage of text from which words have been deleted and replaced with blanks.

The passage will have forty blanks in total, and the goal is to determine the missing words (fill in the blanks) by using the given context clues. Context clues are hints that the author gives to help readers understand the overall meaning of the text. The first and the last sentences of the passage will be complete.

On the exam, there will not be a list of words to choose from—this section is not multiple-choice. The number of letters in each missing word will be given. Each blank space will be composed of dashes; each dash represents one letter of the missing word. For example, if there are four dashes, then the word is four letters long: _ _ _ _.

The word selected will be considered correct only if it is correct in terms of both grammar and meaning. For example, it has to be the *right part of speech* (a verb, a noun, an adjective), and it has to *fit into the sentence* in the right way (plural/singular, past/present).

For some blanks, there will be more than one potential right answer. For others, though, only one word will be the right fit. If more than one word is a potential correct answer, then credit be will received as long as the above criteria are met.

To prepare for the Cloze Test, it's helpful to review the parts of speech to see how they collectively function to form complete sentences (sentences with a subject and a predicate, also called *independent clauses*). Familiarity with parts of speech strengthens one's ability to fill in the blanks of the Cloze exercise correctly.

The Eight Parts of Speech		
Nouns	refer to people, places, things, or ideas	*mother, school, book, beauty*
Pronouns	alternatives for nouns	*I, you, she, it, this*
Verbs	express action or states of being	*run, drive, appear, remember*
Adjectives	modify nouns	*dark blue, average*
Adverbs	modify verbs; answer *when? where? how?* and *why?*	*soon, there, happily, entirely*
Prepositions	express the relationship between a noun and another element	*about, before, through, after*
Coordinating conjunctions	used to connect clauses or sentences or to coordinate words in the same clause	*and, but, for, yet, nor, so*
Interjections	exclamations	*Wow! Hi!*

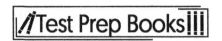

Nouns

A *noun* is a word used to describe a person, place, thing, or idea. They are often the subject, object, or direct object of a sentence. There are five main types of nouns:

- Common nouns
- Proper nouns
- General nouns
- Specific nouns
- Collective nouns

Common nouns are general words that can be used to name people, places, and things:

- People: mom, brother, neighbor
- Places: office, gym, restaurant
- Things: bed, computer, sandwich

Proper nouns are specific words that can be used to name people, places, and things. For example:

- People: Amelia Earhart, Albert Einstein, Stephen Hawking
- Places: Philadelphia, Pennsylvania; Bombay, India; Australia
- Brands: Levi's jeans, Apple computer

Note the difference between common and proper nouns:

- Common noun: The suspect said that she'd eaten breakfast with her sister that morning.
- Proper noun: The suspect said that she'd eaten breakfast with Jane Lowe that morning.

Sometimes common and proper nouns appear in the same sentence:

George Washington was the first *president*.

General nouns are words used to describe conditions or ideas. They are abstract by nature. For example:

- Condition: bravery, love
- Idea: justice, freedom

Specific nouns are words used to describe particular people, places, and things. For example:

- People: victim, perpetrator, officer
- Places: city, beach, stadium
- Things: holster, badge, custody

Collective nouns are words used to refer to groups of people, places, or things as a whole. For example, *flock, group, bunch, crowd, tribe,* and *pack* are all collective nouns.

Pronouns

A *pronoun* is a word that replaces a noun in a sentence. There are seven types:

- Personal
- Reflexive
- Relative
- Interrogative
- Demonstrative
- Indefinite
- Reciprocal

Personal Pronouns

Personal pronouns are words that represent specific people or things (for example, I, you, he, she, me, you, and mine).

Three things must be considered in choosing the correct personal pronoun: *grammatical case, quantity,* and *point of view*.

Grammatical Case

A noun or pronoun's case refers to its relationship to the other words in a sentence. There are three cases of pronouns:

Nominative	nouns and pronouns that are the subject of a verb	I, we, you, he, she, it, they
Objective	nouns and pronouns that are the direct or indirect objects of a verb	Me, us, you, him, her, it, they
Possessive	used to show ownership	Me, mine, ours, your, yours, his, her, hers, its, their

Quantity

When referring to a quantity that is more than, the pronouns must be singular (I, him, you—one person). When referring to a quantity of more than one, the pronoun must be plural (we, their, your—several people).

Point of View

Point of view refers to perspective. There are three types of point of view:

First person refers to the perspective of the person speaking.

> *I* did not do anything.

Second person refers to the perspective of a person being spoken to.

> *You* are a witness.

Third person refers to the perspective of a person being spoken about.

> *The suspect* fled the vicinity.

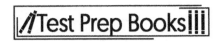

Reflexive Pronouns

Reflexive pronouns are preceded by the adverb, adjective, pronoun, or noun to which they refer. They are used to rename the subjects of action verbs or function as different types of objects: *myself, himself, herself, themselves, yourself, yourselves, ourselves.*

She was in a hurry, so she did the reports *herself.*

Intensive pronouns are reflexive pronouns that are only used to add *emphasis* to the subject of a sentence; they aren't required for meaning: *myself, yourself, himself, herself, itself, ourselves, yourselves,* and *themselves.*

We met the king *himself.*

Relative Pronouns

Relative pronouns are used to connect phrases or clauses to a noun or pronoun. There are eight relative pronouns: *that, which, who, whom, whose, whichever, whoever,* and *whomever.*

The first point of entry was closed, *which* meant we had to enter through the back.

Interrogative Pronouns

Interrogative pronouns are used to ask a question. There are five interrogative pronouns: *what, which, who, whom,* and *whose.*

Whose boots are those?

Special note about *who/whom*: substitute *he* for *who* and *him* for *whom* to determine which should be used.

[Who or whom] wrote that email?

He wrote that email?

Him wrote that email?

He=who, so *who* is correct.

She gave the presentation to [*who* or *whom*]?

She gave the presentation to he?

She gave the presentation to him?

Him=whom, so *whom* is correct.

Demonstrative Pronouns

Demonstrative pronouns take the place of a noun phrase. There are six demonstrative pronouns: *this, that, these, those, none,* and *neither.*

That is not the right thing to do.

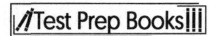

Indefinite Pronouns

Indefinite pronouns are used when referring to a person or thing in a general way. Some examples *include all, another, any, anyone, each, everything, nobody, and several.*

>*Each* is separated by category.

Reciprocal Pronouns

Reciprocal pronouns are used when two or more people have done something simultaneously. The two reciprocal pronouns are: *each other* and *one another.*

>They were kind to *each other.*

Verbs

Verbs are words that express actions or occurrences; they signal the sentence's predicate (what the subject is doing). While a noun is often the subject of a sentence, the verb expresses what is happening or what has happened. For a sentence to be complete, a verb must be included. There are three main types of verbs: *action, linking,* and *helping.*

Action Verbs

Action verbs are verbs that show that something is happening, or that something/someone is in possession of something else.

>Security personnel *detained* the prisoner.

>Detective Suarez *has* a subject in custody.

There are two types of action verbs: transitive and intransitive.

Transitive verbs refer to an object that is receiving the action. There must be a direct object.

>The sergeant apprehended the suspect.

The transitive verb in this sentence is *apprehended. The suspect* is the verb's direct object, that is, that which receives the action. Without the direct object to go along with the transitive verb, the sentence wouldn't make sense: *the sergeant apprehended.* Transitive verbs can be active or passive:

A verb is *active* if the subject of the sentence performs the action. Transitive active verbs are the verbs in sentences with direct objects.

>Officer Lee *pursued* the suspect.

The subject, *Officer Lee,* performed the action, *pursued,* and *the suspect* is the direct object that receives that action.

The verb is *passive* if the subject or direct object is on the receiving end of the action.

>The suspect *was pursued* by Officer Lee.

In this sentence, the subject of the sentence is *the suspect* and it is receiving Officer Lee's action.

Intransitive verbs are action words that don't need direct objects.

> The recruits progressed well.

The verb in this sentence is *progressed*. We know it is an intransitive verb because a direct object (what they progressed in or with) is unnecessary for the sentence to be complete.

Linking Verbs

Linking verbs are verbs that link the subject of the sentence to more information about that subject.

> The altercation *was* verbal.

In this sentence, *the altercation* is the subject, and we learn something new about it—*what kind* of altercation it was. *Was* serves as the verb in this sentence, linking the subject and the added information.

Common Linking Verbs			
is	are	seems	feels
was	become	might	am

Some action verbs can also be linking verbs.

> The defendant *appeared* before the court.

In the sentence above, *appeared* is an action verb.

> The defendant *appeared remorseful* when addressing the judge.

In the sentence above, *appeared* links the defendant to the subject complement, *remorseful.*

Helping Verbs

Helping verbs are words that appear before action or linking verbs. Their purpose is to add information about either time or possibility. The addition of a helping verb to an action or linking verb creates a verb phrase.

> Andrew *is appearing* before the judge.

In this sentence, *Andrew* is the subject, *is* is the helping verb, and *appearing* is the action verb.

Common Helping Verbs			
am	is	are	was
were	be	being	been
have	has	had	do
does	did	done	could
should	would	can	might

Conjugation

Conjugation refers to changing verbs to indicate *point of view, number, tense,* and *mood.* It also refers to subject/verb agreement.

Point of View

Verbs are conjugated to match the point of view of the subject of a sentence.

I *am* a police officer.

In this sentence, *am* is a conjugation of the verb *to be*, for the subject *I*. *I to be a police officer,* or *I are a police officer,* are incorrect.

Number

Verbs are conjugated to indicate how many people are involved in the action of a sentence.

She runs a ten-minute mile.

They run every day.

The verb *to run* is conjugated by adding an *s* to indicate that one person is running. If the action includes more than one person, the conjugation changes: an *s* is not needed.

Tense

The tense of a verb indicates when the action is taking place. There are six possible verb tenses:

- Present: The action is currently happening or happens habitually.
- Past: The action has happened already.
- Future: The action will happen at a later date.
- Present perfect: The action started in the past and continues.
- Past perfect: Two actions occurred in the past, one before the other.
- Future perfect: The action will be complete before another action occurs in the future.

Conjugating a verb so that it is in the present or past tense is as simple as changing the form through letter addition or substitution. For the other tenses, including future, present perfect, past perfect, and future perfect, a helping verb is required.

Present: I run.	*Present perfect*: I have run.
Past: I ran.	*Past perfect*: I had run.
Future: I will run.	*Future perfect*: I will have run.

Mood

The *mood* indicates the purpose of a sentence and the speaker's general attitude. There are five common moods:

- Indicative: used for facts, opinions, and questions.

    The officer wrote a ticket. ← This is a statement of fact.

- Imperative: used for orders and requests.

    Put your hands on the vehicle. ← This is an order.

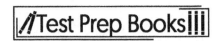

- Interrogative: used for questioning.

    Will you stand down? ← This is a question.

- Conditional: used in a "what if" conditional state that will cause something else to happen.

    I might break my arm if I slip on the ice. ← This is a "what if" causal scenario.

- Subjunctive: used for wishes and other statements that are doubtful or not factual.

    I wish that no one used drugs. ← This expresses a wish.

Voice

The voice of a verb is active if the subject of the sentence is performing the action. If the subject is on the receiving end of the action, the verb is passive. See also *transitive verbs*.

Adjectives

An *adjective* is a word used to modify or describe a noun or pronoun. By answering questions about the noun or pronoun, adjectives make a sentence more specific. An adjective usually answers one of three questions:

- Which one?

    The *older* brother was seen entering the building.

    In this sentence, the *brother* is the subject. The adjective, *older*, tells us which one.

- What kind?

    Professional officers can become detectives.

    In this sentence, the adjective, *professional*, tells us what kind of officer can become a detective.

- How many or how often?

    She drinks milk *five* times a day.

    In this sentence, the adjective, *five*, tells us how many times a day the person drinks milk.

Articles

Another type of adjective is an *article*, which is used to identify a noun in a sentence. There are three articles in the English language: *the, a,* and *an. The* is a *definite* article, and *a* and *an* are *indefinite* articles, so it's important to choose the right one for meaning.

The is used when there is a limited number (definite) of something being referred to.

    I left *the book* on the couch.

In this sentence, the noun being referred to is *book*. Choosing the article *the* indicates that one particular book was left on the couch.

71

A and *an* are used when there is not a fixed amount (indefinite) of something being referred to.

> I left *a book* on the couch.

Again, the noun in the sentence is *book.* The article changed to *a* because the sentence no longer refers to one specific book.

On the Cloze Test, it will be important to remember that *an* comes before nouns that begin with a vowel.

> I left *an old* book on the couch.

Comparisons

Adjectives can also be used to make comparisons. These adjectives come in two forms: relative and absolute.

Relative adjectives show a comparison between two things. There are three degrees of relative adjectives: *positive*, *comparative*, and *superlative.*

- Positive: the base form of the adjective

    The painting was *beautiful.*

- *Comparative*: a higher level of some quality of the adjective

    The painting was *more* beautiful than I expected it to be.

- *Superlative*: The highest form of quality of the adjective

    The painting was the *most beautiful* painting I've ever seen.

Absolute adjectives also show comparison, but not in varying degrees; they're *non-gradable.* A good example of an absolute adjective is *empty.* If there are two boxes, and one of them is *empty,* the other box cannot be *emptier, more emptier,* or *most empty.* The box is either empty or it is not. *Empty* is an absolute adjective.

Adverbs

An *adverb* is a word or phrase that modifies verbs, adjectives, or other adverbs. Like adjectives, adverbs are also words that can be used to answer questions. Adverbs answer the following:

- When? She drove *yesterday.*
- Where? They drove *here.*
- How? He drove *quickly.*
- To what extent? She drives *whenever possible.*
- Why? We ride the bus *to avoid traffic.*

As seen in the examples, some adverbs end in *–ly,* but not all. The words *not* and *never* are considered adverbs because they modify adjectives.

Again, like adjectives, adverbs can be used to make comparisons in three degrees: *positive, comparative,* and *superlative.*

- They *quietly* went into the building.
- The squad went into the building *more quietly* than the cadets.
- The squad leader went into the building *most quietly.*

Prepositions

A *preposition* is a word that appears in a sentence to show the relationship between a noun or pronoun and another element.

> The books are *on* the shelves.

The preposition, *on,* shows the relationship between the books (noun) and the shelves (another noun).

Common Prepositions				
aboard	behind	during	outside	to
about	below	for	over	toward
above	beyond	inside	past	under
among	by	into	since	upon
around	despite	near	through	within

Conjunctions

Conjunctions join pieces of words, phrases, or clauses. There are three types of conjunctions: *coordinating, correlative,* and *subordinating.*

Coordinating Conjunctions
Coordinating conjunctions connect equal parts of sentences. Common coordinating conjunctions are *for, and, nor, but, or, yet, so* (sometimes called the FANBOYS).

> The poem was brief, *but* it was beautiful.

In this sentence *but* connects two independent clauses into one sentence.

In some cases, coordinating conjunctions convey a sense of contrast. In the example above, the poem's beauty is in contrast to the length of it.

Correlative Conjunctions
Correlative conjunctions show the connection between pairs. Common correlative conjunctions are *either/or, neither/nor, not only/but also, both/and, whether/or,* and *so/as.*

> *Either* you're having lunch at home, *or* you're eating out.

In this sentence, *either* and *or* are used to connect two options.

Subordinating Conjunctions

Subordinating conjunctions join dependent clauses with independent clauses, providing a transition between two ideas. This transition often adds information about time, place, or the effect of something.

Our team lost the game *because* Jim was unprepared.

In this sentence, *because* is connecting two clauses and indicating a cause and effect relationship between them.

Common Subordinating Conjunctions		
after	since	whenever
although	so that	where
because	unless	wherever
before	when	in order that

Interjections

An *interjection* is an exclamatory word used to indicate extreme emotion or feeling. Some examples include *Hey! Oh!* and *Wow!*

These words can be used alone as a complete sentence, or they can be added to a sentence to indicate a forceful change in thought or add feeling.

Wow! You look great today!

Hey, in my opinion, he deserves the presidency.

In the first sentence, *Wow!* is the interjection used to add feeling to the speaker's opinion. In the second sentence, the speaker uses *Hey* to grab the listener's attention before expressing their opinion.

Practice Questions

Instructions: In the fictional narrative below, wherever you see a dashed blank line, you have to supply the correct word. The dashes equal the number of letters in the missing word. For a word to be considered correct, it must make sense in the passage, and it must have the same number of letters as there are dashes.

There may be a break in the biggest, most perplexing art heist case of the past thirty years. The Federal Bureau of Investigation (FBI) told reporters (1) _ _ _ _ _ that video footage from the time of the robbery has been discovered. In 1985, paintings valued at over $400 million were (2) _ _ _ _ _ _ from the Fine (3) _ _ _ _ Museum. The stolen works were considered to be some of the most important of the museum's collection and included (4) _ _ _ _ _ _ _ _ _ by Rembrandt, Manet, Van Gogh, and Vermeer.

It was Thursday, July 8, 1985 when a man dressed as a teacher entered the museum after hours. (5) _ _ told the museum's two security (6) _ _ _ _ _ _ that he believed a (7) _ _ _ _ _ had been separated from his school group during the museum's closing. The guards, (8) _ _ _ had noticed several (9) _ _ _ _ _ _ groups touring the museum that day, thought it was plausible that a child could have been (10) _ _ _ _ behind. They allowed the (11) _ _ _ _ _ _ _, who was in a panic, to accompany them through the halls of the museum, where they called to the missing (12) _ _ _ _ _ _ _. It was then that the teacher managed to detain the (13) _ _ _ _ _ _ in a closet, binding their hands and feet with duct tape.

The guards managed to free (14) _ _ _ _ _ _ _ _ _ _ in what they estimated after the fact to be (15) _ _ _ _ _ _ _ _ _ _ _ _ _ ten minutes. They quickly summoned the police and locked down the museum in accordance with robbery protocols. In just that period of ten (16) _ _ _ _ _ _ _, eight paintings were (17) _ _ _ _ _ _. At the time of the investigation, this led police and investigators from the FBI's Art Theft Division to estimate that at least three (18) _ _ _ _ _ _ _ must have been involved. This estimation was later called (19) _ _ _ _ question after a journalist suggested that the guards' sense of (20) _ _ _ _ might have been off due to the stress of the situation. If the guards were detained for more than ten minutes, (21) _ _ _ _ _ than three thieves could have taken the paintings. Alternatively, if the guards were detained for less than ten minutes, (22) _ _ _ _ than three thieves would have been needed to gain access to the museum.

At the time of the heist, the Chicago Police Department and the FBI both (23) _ _ _ _ _ _ _ that the art would be recovered when the thieves (24) _ _ _ _ _ _ _ _ _ to sell it, as often occurs when very famous works are stolen. Flash-forward more than thirty years, and the art has still (25) _ _ _ to surface. The (26) _ _ _ _ _ _ of time that the thieves have remained at large is not the only unique thing about this case, (27) _ _ _ _ _ _. There have been a number of red herrings, the most notable being the lengthy inquiry into and subsequent arrest of (28) _ _ _ _ _ _ _ men who had installed protective glass in that wing of the museum just a few (29) _ _ _ _ _ prior to the robbery. Though two service men from Anderson Glass were arrested, due to insufficient evidence, namely the paintings (30) _ _ _ _ _ _ _ _ _ _, the U.S. Attorney was unable to (31) _ _ _ _ _ their guilt.

The announcement today that new evidence had been (32) _ _ _ _ _ _ _ _ _ was a shock to many, the FBI included. In a joint statement made by the FBI and the Justice Department, U.S. Attorney Maria Lopez (33) _ _ _ _, "This is the kind of break we always hope for when a case has gone cold." The video footage is not from the museum's security system, but from a convenience store down the street from the museum. The store, Grab'n'Go, has been owned by the same family for forty-five years.

"When my father passed away over the winter, we started to clean out his office at the back of the store," said Casey Initeri, the current (34) _ _ _ _ _ and operator of the store.

"What we found were stacks of old VHS tapes from the store's (35) _ _ _ _ _ _ _ _ camera. My father had a big box of them and would record over old tapes whenever he needed to. (36) _ just saw an article in the paper about the 30th anniversary of the (37) _ _ _ _ _, so the date was on my mind when I saw that the label on one of Dad's tapes read July, 1985. I couldn't believe it. I called the FBI right away."

The FBI has not yet disclosed to the press the (38) _ _ _ _ _ _ _ _ of the tape, so how it will advance the case is still unknown. The thieves (39) _ _ _ _ _ _ approached or retreated from the museum past the convenience store, so it is likely that their vehicle (and maybe even their faces) are on the tape.

Empty frames currently (40) _ _ _ _ on the walls of the Chicago Fine Arts Museum in an eerie testament to the works that were taken. That wing of the museum has become a place not to learn about art, but to speculate about a perfect crime.

Answer Explanations

1. today

2. stolen

3. Arts

4. paintings

5. He

6. guards

7. child

8. who

9. school

10. left

11. teacher

12. student

13. guards

14. themselves

15. approximately

16. minutes

17. taken

18. thieves

19. into

20. time

21. fewer

22. more

23. assumed

24. attempted

25. yet

26. amount

27. though

28. service

29. weeks

30. themselves

31. prove

32. uncovered

33. said

34. owner

35. security

36. I

37. heist/crime

38. contents

39. either

40. hang

Reasoning

Law enforcement officers use their powers of observation to gather information. Through their reasoning skill-sets, they'll make inferences and draw conclusions about information and evidence.

Very broadly, reasoning is an approach to thinking that prioritizes logic. Law enforcement officers use reasoning every day when forming judgments about suspects, piecing together timelines, and evaluating crime scenes.

There are three types of reasoning problems on the California POST:

- Comparative Values
- Numerical Series
- Similar Words

There will be sixteen total Reasoning items on the exam. These items require searches for patterns, similarities, and relationships in order to choose the correct answer. There will be lists of statements, numbers, or words, and test takers will analyze the given information in order to answer the question.

Comparative Values

A *comparative value* item provides details about specific subjects, like types of fruit or family members, and then asks that comparisons be drawn between them. There are two possible tasks:

- Order the subjects from least to greatest or greatest to least
- Find *the value* of a certain subject

When encountering a comparative value item, it's helpful to make a list and fill it in according to information given in the prompt. Everything needed to answer this type of question correctly is in the question. Here's an example:

> A vehicle rental company stocks cars, vans, busses, and trucks. The company ranks their vehicles by popularity so that they know what to buy when expanding their business. Cars are ranked between vans and trucks. Trucks are more popular than vans. Buses are ranked lowest. Which type of vehicle is rented the most?
>
> a. Cars
> b. Vans
> c. Busses
> d. Trucks

C   V   T   B

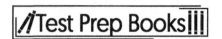

The items being compared are the prompt's subjects. In this question, there are cars, vans, buses, and trucks. Assigning them a letter or an image, as illustrated above, is a helpful way to list them quickly. For this question, the first letter of each vehicle represents the subject: C (car), V (van), T (truck), and B (bus).

Note what the prompt actually asks. In this prompt, the goal is to find which vehicle is rented *the most*. Thus the list needs to be ordered from *most to least*:

Vehicles Rented – Most to Least

Determine which information is stated outright, meaning it is known for sure. In this prompt, *buses are ranked the lowest,* so buses can be placed at the bottom of the list:

Vehicles Rented – Most to Least
B

Next, look through the prompt for more information. This prompt states that *cars are ranked between vans and trucks*, so the list can look one of two ways:

Vehicles Rented – Most to Least Possibility 1	Vehicles Rented – Most to Least Possibility 2
V	T
C	C
T	V
B	B

To decide which list is correct, look for the last piece of information given in the prompt. In this prompt, *trucks are more popular than vans.* Which one of the lists shows that to be true?

Vehicles Rented – Most to Least
T
C
V
B

Revisit the final question to determine the response. *Which vehicle is being rented the most?* The answer is *D*, Trucks.

Numerical Series

A *numerical series* item presents a list of numbers and asks test takers to determine what the next number should be. The key to answering this type of question correctly is to understand *the relationship between the numbers* in the series. Do they increase or decrease, and at what rate? Is there a pattern? Here's an example:

> Identify the next number in the series: 7, 14, 21, 28, 35, ...
> a. 42
> b. 28
> c. 47
> d. 50

First, decide if the numbers in the list are *increasing* or *decreasing*. Generally, if numbers increase, it is indicative of addition or multiplication. If they decrease, subtraction or division is more likely.

The numbers in this list are *increasing*: 7, 14, 21, 28, 35.

Here's a strategy to determine *the rate* at which they are increasing:

7,   14,   21,   28,   35

+7   +7   +7   +7

The numbers in the list are increasing by 7. The rate of increase is constant throughout the list. Note that not all lists will increase or decrease at a constant rate.

To find the answer to this question, simply continue the rate of increase by adding 7 to 35. The answer is *A*, 42.

Here's a more complicated example:

> Identify the next number in the series: 2, 3, 5, 9, 17...
> a. 24
> b. 33
> c. 37
> d. 39

Again, the first thing to do is decide if the numbers in the list are increasing or decreasing. The numbers in this list are *increasing*: 2, 3, 5, 9, 17.

Next, figure out the rate of increase:

2,   3,   5,   9,   17

+1   +2   +4   +8

Notice that, in this question, the rate of increase is not constant. The question needs to be solved by looking for a pattern in the rate of increase.

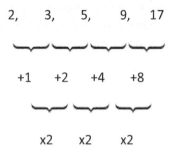

2,   3,   5,   9,   17

+1   +2   +4   +8

x2   x2   x2

1, 2, 4, and 8 are all *multiples of 2*: 1 x 2 = 2, 2 x 2 = 4, 4 x 2 = 8. What is needed to continue this pattern? *8 x 2.*

Given that 8 x 2 = 16, 16 is the next number in the rate of increase.

2,   3,   5,   9,   17

+1   +2   +4   +8   +16

x2   x2   x2   x2

So, 16 must be added to the last number in the list to find the answer: 17 + 16 = 33. The answer is *B*, 33.

Similar Words

In *similar words* questions, there will be a set of four words. Three of the words will be similar, and one will be different. The goal is to choose the one word that is *unlike* the other three.

The key to answering these questions correctly is to e*stablish the relationship between the three similar words.* The word that does not share that relationship with the others will be the answer. Here's an example:

Three of the following words are similar, while one is different. Select the word that is different.
a. Pants
b. Closet
c. Dresses
d. Skirts

First, consider what the *theme* of the words is. The theme of this list seems to be *clothing.* Next, start with Choice *A* and consider how this word relates to choice *B*. Pants can *be kept* in a closet.

In Choices *C* and *D*, dresses and skirts, like pants, can also be kept in a closet. So, three out of four of the words are articles of clothing that can be kept in a closet, rendering *closet* the word that is unlike the others. The answer is *B*, Closet.

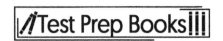

Here's another example:

Three of the following words are similar, while one is different. Select the word that is different.

    a. Book
    b. Magazine
    c. Newspaper
    d. Reading

In this question, the theme is *reading*, which is also one of the answer choices. Choices *A*, *B*, and *C* are things that can be read. Though choice *D*, reading, does relate to the other answer choices, it does not relate in the same way. Reading is a verb, not an object that can be read, so the word that does not belong is D, Reading.

Practice Questions

Directions: Officers often face situations in which they need to determine how different pieces of information relate to one another. In this section, you will be presented with information, such as a group or ordered series of facts, numbers, letters, or words. Your task is to study the various pieces of information and try to understand how they relate to one another. Mark the letter that identifies your choice on your answer sheet.

1. Three of the following words are similar, while one is different. Which one is different?
   a. Student
   b. Teacher
   c. Desk
   d. Principal

2. The families who live on Gardenia Drive keep dogs, cats, and rabbits as pets. There are 3 more cats than dogs. There are 5 more dogs than rabbits. There are 2 rabbits. How many cats live on Gardenia Drive?
   a. 10
   b. 4
   c. 2
   d. 11

3. Which of the following is the next number in the series: 2, 13, 4, 14, 8, 15...?
   a. 16
   b. 17
   c. 32
   d. 14

4. A local librarian conducts a poll to gauge what types of baked goods should be sold at the library fundraiser. Cookies are ranked between cakes and pies. Pies are ranked higher than cakes. Cream puffs receive the least number of votes. Which type of baked goods receives the most votes?
   a. Cookies
   b. Cakes
   c. Pies
   d. Cream puffs

5. Three of the following words are similar, while one is different. Which one is different?
   a. Roof
   b. Skylight
   c. Ceiling
   d. Floor

6. Which of the following is the next number in the series: 84, 80, 76, 72, 68...?
   a. 75
   b. 67
   c. 64
   d. 70

7. Which of the following is the next number in the series: 17, 18, 20, 23, 27...?
   a. 29
   b. 33
   c. 23
   d. 32

8. After school, Andrew, Matt and Geeta spend time watching television. Andrew watches more television than Geeta, but less than Matt. Which of the following lists from most to least the friends in order of how much television they watch after school?
   a. Andrew, Matt, Geeta
   b. Not enough information
   c. Geeta, Andrew, Matt
   d. Matt, Andrew, Geeta

9. Three of the following words are similar, while one is different. Which one is different?
   a. Notebook
   b. Pencil
   c. Pen
   d. Crayon

10. Which of the following is the next number in the series: 41, 30, 42, 29, 43, 28...?
    a. 30
    b. 44
    c. 43
    d. 41

11. Alejandro, Jennifer and Walt are competing in their track team's 500-meter dash. Jennifer finished behind Walt but ahead of Alejandro. Who won the race?
    a. Alejandro
    b. Jennifer
    c. Walt
    d. Not enough information

12. Which of the following is the next number in the series: 144, 133, 130, 119, 116...?
    a. 113
    b. 105
    c. 127
    d. 98

13. Three of the following words are similar, while one is different. Which one is different?
    a. Lake
    b. Ocean
    c. River
    d. Boat

14. Which of the following is the next number in the series: 288, 144, 72, 36, 18...?
    a. 4
    b. 12
    c. 6
    d. 9

15. On their driving test, Anna earned 97 points, 12 points more than Michael. Michael scored 10 points higher than Tom, who scored 6 points lower than Jaime. What was Tom's score?

    a. 109

    b. 22

    c. 75

    d. 91

16. Which of the following is the next number in the series: 3, 9, 27, 81, 243...?

    a. 486

    b. 729

    c. 121

    d. 356

Answer Explanations

1. C: The word *desk* is not like the other three. A student, teacher, and principal are all people who are found in a school setting. A desk is an inanimate object that can be found in a school setting, rendering it different from the other three words.

2. A: The correct answer is 10. According to the prompt, there are 2 rabbits on Gardenia Drive. If there are 5 more dogs than rabbits, then there are 7 dogs. If there are 3 more cats than dogs, then 10 cats live on Gardenia Drive.

3. A: The next number in the series is 16. In this series, two patterns of increase can be found. Every other number either doubles or increases by one. So, to find the next number in the series, decide which pattern the missing number should continue. Because 2x2 is 4 and 4x2 is 8, the missing number is 16.

4. C: The correct answer is pies. According to the prompt, cookies are ranked between cakes and pies, and pies are ranked higher than cakes. At this point, the list should read *pies, cookies,* and *cakes*. The last information in the prompt is that cream puffs received the least number of votes, so *pies* remains at the top of the list, having the most votes received.

5. D: The word *floor* is not like the other three. A roof, skylight, and ceiling are all elements of a house or building positioned *above*. The floor is positioned *below*, making it unlike the other three words.

6. C: The next number in the series is 64. In this series, each successive number is 4 less than the number that preceded it. So, to find the next number in the series, subtract 4 from the previous number.

7. D: The next number in the series is 32. In this series, the numbers increase by *one more with each successive number*. So, there is an increase of 1 between the first two numbers, an increase of 2 between the second and third numbers, an increase of 3 between the third and fourth numbers, and an increase of 4 between the fourth and fifth numbers. The next number in the series should be 5 more than the last number given.

8. D: The correct answer is Matt, Andrew, Geeta. According to the prompt, Andrew watches more television than Geeta. Since the goal is to rank the friends in order of how much television they watch *from most to least*, the list should read the following way so far: Andrew, Geeta. The prompt goes on to say that Andrew watches less television than Matt, so Matt must be added to the list above Andrew.

9. A: The word *notebook* is not like the other three. A pencil, pen, and crayon can all be used to write or draw. A notebook is something that is written or drawn *in*, rendering it different from the other three words.

10. B: The next number in the series is 44. Beginning with the first number in the series, every other number *increases by 1*. Beginning with the second number, every other number *decreases by 1*. So, to find the next number in the series, decide which pattern the missing number should continue. The missing number should continue the pattern of increasing by 1 starting with the first number in the series. Looking only at that pattern, the series reads 41...42...43. Continuing that pattern, the missing number should be 44.

11. D: Out of the three on this particular team, Walt came in first. However, it's unclear whether or not other teams were participating in this race. Thus, there is insufficient information to determine whether or not Walt won the race.

12. B: The next number in the series is 105. In this series, the numbers are decreasing. The gap between each number is either 11 or 3. Following this pattern, the next number should be 11 less than the last number.

13. D: The word *boat* is not like the other three. A lake, ocean, and river are all bodies of water. A boat is a vessel used to traverse bodies of water, rendering it different from the other three words.

14. D: The next number in the series is 9. In this series, each successive number decreases by half.

15. C: Tom's score was 75. According to the prompt, Anna earned 97 points, which was 12 more than Michael. Michael earned 85 points, which is 10 more than Tom.

16. B: The next number in the series is 729. In this series, each number is multiplied by 3 to get the next number, so the next number would be 243 x 3, which is 729.

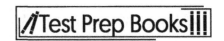

Dear California Post Test Taker,

We would like to start by thanking you for purchasing this study guide for your California Post exam. We hope that we exceeded your expectations.

Our goal in creating this study guide was to cover all of the topics that you will see on the test. We also strove to make our practice questions as similar as possible to what you will encounter on test day. With that being said, if you found something that you feel was not up to your standards, please send us an email and let us know.

We have study guides in a wide variety of fields. If you're interested in one, try searching for it on Amazon or send us an email.

Thanks Again and Happy Testing!
Product Development Team
info@studyguideteam.com

FREE Test Taking Tips DVD Offer

To help us better serve you, we have developed a Test Taking Tips DVD that we would like to give you for FREE. **This DVD covers world-class test taking tips that you can use to be even more successful when you are taking your test.**

All that we ask is that you email us your feedback about your study guide. Please let us know what you thought about it – whether that is good, bad or indifferent.

To get your **FREE Test Taking Tips DVD**, email freedvd@studyguideteam.com with "FREE DVD" in the subject line and the following information in the body of the email:

     a. The title of your study guide.

     b. Your product rating on a scale of 1-5, with 5 being the highest rating.

     c. Your feedback about the study guide. What did you think of it?

     d. Your full name and shipping address to send your free DVD.

If you have any questions or concerns, please don't hesitate to contact us at freedvd@studyguideteam.com.

Thanks again!

Made in the USA
Las Vegas, NV
26 November 2023

81580410R00057